# Martin Luther King, Jr.

*with profiles of*
Mohandas K. Gandhi
*and* Nelson Mandela

World Book, Inc.
a Scott Fetzer company
Chicago

# BIOGRAPHICAL ⊕ CONNECTIONS

Writer: Lori Meek Schuldt.

World Book, Inc.
233 N. Michigan Ave.
Chicago, IL 60601

For information about other World Book publications, visit our Web site at **www.worldbook.com** or call **1-800-WORLDBK (967-5325)**.
For information about sales to schools and libraries, call **1-800-975-3250 (United States)**, or **1-800-837-5365 (Canada)**.

**Library of Congress Cataloging-in-Publication Data**

Schuldt, Lori Meek.
   Martin Luther King, Jr.: with profiles of Mohandas K. Gandhi and Nelson Mandela / [writer, Lori Meek Schuldt].
      p. cm. -- (Biographical connections)
   Summary: "A biography of Martin Luther King, Jr., with profiles of two prominent individuals, associated through the influences they had on one another, the successes they achieved, or the goals they worked toward. Includes recommended readings and web sites"--Provided by publisher.
Includes bibliographical references and index.
   ISBN-13: 978-0-7166-1822-5
   ISBN-10: 0-7166-1822-2
   1. King, Martin Luther, Jr., 1929-1968--Juvenile literature. 2. African Americans--Biography--Juvenile literature. 3. Civil rights workers--United States--Biography--Juvenile literature. 4. Baptists--United States--Clergy--Biography--Juvenile literature. 5. African Americans--Civil rights--History--20th century--Juvenile literature. 6. Civil rights movements--United States--History--20th century--Juvenile literature. 7. Gandhi, Mahatma, 1869-1948--Juvenile literature. 8. Mandela, Nelson, 1918---Juvenile literature.  I. World Book, Inc. II. Title. III. Series.
E185.97.K5S366 2007
323.092'2--dc22
[B]
                             2006011024

Printed in the United States of America
1  2  3  4  5  10  09  08  07  06

# Contents

# Acknowledgments

The publisher gratefully acknowledges the following sources for the photographs in this volume.

| | |
|---|---|
| Cover: | © Corbis/Bettmann; |
| | © AlexanderJoe, AFP/Getty Images; |
| | © Corbis/Bettmann |
| 7 | © Corbis/Bettmann |
| 10-14 | AP/Wide World |
| 21 | © Corbis/Hulton-Deutsch |
| 22 | © Time & Life Pictures/Getty Images |
| 25 | © Flip Schulke, Corbis |
| 26 | © Corbis/Bettmann |
| 28 | © Flip Schulke/Corbis |
| 31 | © Corbis/Bettmann |
| 38 | © Flip Schulke, Corbis |
| 41 | © Donald Uhrbrock, Time & Life Pictures/Getty Images |
| 49 | © Corbis/Bettmann |
| 51 | © Time & Life Pictures/Getty Images |
| 52 | © Hulton Archive, Getty Images |
| 57 | © Jack Moebes, Corbis |
| 67 | © Corbis/Hulton-Deutsch |
| 71-78 | © Corbis/Bettmann |
| 87 | © AFP/Getty Images |
| 89 | © Alexander Joe, AFP/Getty Images |
| 99-107 | AP/Wide World |

# Preface

*Biographical Connections* takes a contextual approach in presenting the lives of important people. In each volume, there is a biography of a central figure. This biography is preceded and followed by profiles of other individuals whose lifework connects in some way to that of the central figure. The three subjects are associated through the influences they had on one another, the successes they achieved, or the goals they worked toward. The series includes men and women from around the world and throughout history in a variety of fields.

This volume presents as its central figure the African American civil rights activist Martin Luther King, Jr., whose leadership during the 1950's and 1960's helped legally abolish long-standing racial segregation in the South. King's biography is preceded by a profile of the Indian leader Mohandas K. Gandhi, who developed a nonviolent method of direct social action that helped India win its independence from the United Kingdom in the 1940's. Gandhi's method was used by both King and the black South African leader Nelson Mandela, the subject of the profile that follows King's biography. Mandela's struggle against the white-minority government's policy of rigid racial separation paralleled King's struggle for civil rights but lasted much longer, into the 1990's.

All three of these great leaders were born into environments in which white people of European extraction held power and treated those whose skin was darker as less than equal human beings. Gandhi, King, and Mandela could each recount humiliating incidents early in their own lives in which they suffered a loss of dignity because of racial discrimination. Although none of them initially set out to rid the world of social injustice, they simply could not stand living with it. Sacrificing their physical safety and the comforts of daily life at home with their families, Gandhi, King, and Mandela overcame their own fears and went on to lead vast groups of disenfranchised citizens in a peaceful effort to regain their dignity and acquire the basic human rights they had been long denied. Each leader was successful in part because of his personal charisma and in part because he spent a great deal of his time reading and listening to the ideas of others, reflecting thoughtfully, and seeking ways to build *consensus* (agreement in opinion) among the parties in dispute.

Underlying Gandhi's and King's practice of nonviolent protest was a deep spiritual belief in the moral rightness of equality. Mandela, on the other hand, regarded nonviolence primarily as a strategic tactic rather than an unyielding principle—a tactic he reluctantly abandoned in the wake of the South African government's vicious response to the initial peaceful protests he led. However, despite the fact that Mandela temporarily resorted to *guerrilla* (warfare conducted by roving bands of fighters) tactics to force the South African government to change, the transfer of power from an all-white to a multiracial government was relatively nonviolent and came through a legitimate election rather than a coup. Mandela—unlike Gandhi and King, who were shot down before their work was completed—lived to enjoy the fruits of his labor, ascending to the presidency of the fractured nation he spent his life fighting to repair. ■

# Mohandas K. Gandhi (1869–1948)

Mohandas Karamchand Gandhi *(Moh huhn DAHS kur uhm CHUHND GAHN dee* or *GAN dee)* was a pioneer in the use of nonviolent resistance to bring about social change. His unique method of direct social action, called *Satyagraha,* helped free India from British control and later inspired leaders in other parts of the world—including Martin Luther King, Jr., in the United States and Nelson Mandela in South Africa—in their campaigns for social justice.

Gandhi is honored by the people of India as the father of their nation. They called Gandhi the *Mahatma* (Great Soul). His life was guided by a search for truth. He believed truth could be known only through tolerance and concern for others and that finding a truthful way to solutions required constant testing. He called his autobiography *The Story of My Experiments with Truth*.

## CHILDHOOD AND MARRIAGE

Gandhi was born on Oct. 2, 1869, in Porbandar, India. This village was the capital of a small *princely state,* also called Porbandar, located on the Kathiawar Peninsula along the northern coast of the Arabian Sea, in the larger Indian state of Gujarat. Gandhi's parents belonged to a *Vaisya* (merchant and professional) caste of Hindus. A *caste* is a social class to which a person belongs by birth. Within a caste, most people share the same culture or occupation, follow the same religious customs, or enjoy the same level of wealth.

At the time Gandhi was born, the caste system in India had been in place for more than 3,000 years. It rigidly controlled Indian society by ranking the social position of the people. Ancient Hindu texts described four main castes, called *varnas*. The *Brahmans* (priests and scholars) were the highest-ranking caste, followed by the *Kshatriyas* (rulers and warriors), *Vaisyas*, and *Sudras* (artisans, laborers, and servants). Over time, each of the four varnas came to include many smaller castes called *jatis*. People in a fifth category, a group considered outside the varnas and of the lowest social status, were commonly called *untouchables* because some upper-caste people believed they would be polluted by the touch of members of this group. Untouchables traditionally held the most undesirable jobs, such as the disposal of garbage or the cleaning of toilets. Strict rules governed behavior between the castes. For example, members of each caste neither married nor dined with members of lower-ranked castes.

Mohandas's father, Karamchand Uttamchand Gandhi, known more familiarly as Kaba Gandhi, followed in the footsteps of his father (Mohandas's grandfather) when in 1847 he became the chief adviser, called a prime minister, to the ruler of Porbandar. But the local rulers of Porbandar and more than 500 other princely states were actually controlled by the British government. The United Kingdom had been the leading European power in India since the 1600's, chiefly through the East India Company, a British trading company that gradually took over much of India's land. In 1858, the United Kingdom took direct control of the East India Company's possessions, which became known as British India. By 1859, after defeating a widespread rebellion in northern and central India, the British controlled nearly all of India either directly or indirectly. Kaba Gandhi outlived each of his first three wives and was in his 40's when he married his fourth wife, Putlibai. They had a daughter, Raliatbehn, and three sons: Laxmidas, Karsandas, and finally Mohandas. When Mohandas was about 7, his family left Porbandar and moved to the city of Rajkot farther inland, where Kaba had taken a similar position as chief adviser to the ruler there. At the age of about 11, Mohandas entered Alfred High School in Rajkot. He began to learn English during his first year at this school. In the upper grades, classes in all subjects were taught in English. Gandhi had grown up speaking Gujarati, a regional native language belonging to the Indo-Aryan language group of northern India, and he found the new language a challenge to learn.

Young Mohandas was a shy, serious boy. He worked hard at school, but he struggled through the multiplication tables and was afraid to talk with his classmates. He was too shy to participate in such sports as cricket or soccer, but he developed a habit of taking long walks in the open air—a habit that would last the rest of his life.

Gandhi's mother was a deeply religious person. A follower of the Vaishnava form of Hinduism, she went to the Vaishnava temple every day and fasted regularly as a sign of her devotion. In accordance with Vaishnava beliefs, she prepared only vegetarian meals for the family. Among the many non-Hindu friends the boy's father welcomed as visitors to the family home were Jains, Muslims, and Parsis (also known as Zoroastrians). Thus, Gandhi grew up in a household with parents who provided examples of both devotion to one's own religion and tolerance for other religions.

According to Hindu custom in India, parents arranged the marriages of their children, who often wed at a young age. Gandhi was 13 years old when in 1882 he married Kasturbai Makanji, a girl about the same age, in a lavish triple wedding ceremony that also included Gandhi's brother Karsandas and a male cousin with their brides. During the early years of their marriage, Mohandas and Kasturbai spent much of their time apart, each living at their own parents' homes.

As a teen-ager, Gandhi had a number of experiences that contributed to the development of his personal values. Early in his teen years, he yearned for greater independence from his elders. In defiance of their restrictions, he and a cousin secretly tried smoking, first by collecting an uncle's cigarette butts and then by buying cheap cigarettes with coins stolen from the servants. Yet they still felt so unbearably frustrated at not being allowed to do anything without their elders' permission that they decided they would kill themselves by swallowing poisonous seeds. But they were afraid to go through with the plan. As he later reflected in his autobiography, Gandhi "realized that it was not as easy to commit suicide as to contemplate it."[1] After this incident, he gave up smoking.

Gandhi also continued to struggle with his childhood fears of the dark and of thieves, ghosts, and serpents. He envied an older, bigger,

*Gandhi poses with his wife, Kasturbai, on their return to India from South Africa in 1915. The couple were married in 1882.*

Muslim boy at school who claimed that eating meat made him strong and brave. To overcome his fears, Gandhi decided to secretly try eating meat even though it was against his family's religious beliefs. This experiment failed. Eating meat did not make him any stronger or braver, and he felt guilty about deceiving his parents. He wrote out a confession of his meat-eating and stealing and handed it to his father, who quietly read it, wept, and forgave him. Gandhi felt that his father's tears washed away his sin. As he later recalled the profound effect this incident had on him, he concluded, "This was, for me, an object-lesson in *ahimsa* [nonviolence]. Then I could read in it nothing more than a father's love, but today I know that it was pure *ahimsa*. When such *ahimsa* becomes all-embracing, it transforms everything it touches. There is no limit to its power."[2]

In November 1885, Gandhi's father died after a lengthy illness. The 16-year-old Gandhi soon afterward suffered a second loss. His wife gave birth to the couple's first child, but the baby died within a few days. Gandhi continued his studies and graduated from high school in late 1887. He then enrolled at Samaldas College in Bhavnagar. His wife, who was pregnant, stayed behind in Rajkot and gave birth to a son, Harilal. Gandhi missed his family and returned home after one semester. The couple would later have three more sons: Manilal, Ramdas, and Devadas.

## EDUCATION AND LAW CAREER

Gandhi was interested in studying medicine, but his family persuaded him to pursue a law degree instead so that he could follow his father's career path. A family friend who was a Brahman suggested that Gandhi study in London. Gandhi was delighted at the idea, but the leader of the caste group in his community warned him that he would be declared *outcaste* (a Hindu who has been excluded from the caste) if he went to England, because their religion forbade voyages abroad. Gandhi chose to go to London anyway and ignored the caste's declaration. He was more concerned with gaining the permission and blessings of his mother, who gave them after he vowed not to touch wine, women, or meat. Gandhi sailed alone for the long voyage to England from Bombay (now Mumbai) on Sept. 4, 1888.

On Nov. 6, 1888, Gandhi began his studies at the Inner Temple, one of the four Inns of Court law schools. In addition to his law courses, Gandhi studied Latin, French, and physics. He also undertook a personal study of the *Bhagavad-Gita,* a philosophical work that is part of Hindu sacred writings, and of the Christian Bible.

In London, Gandhi wore fashionable English clothes. At first, he tried to become more like an English gentleman by taking lessons in dance, violin, and *elocution*—the art of speaking clearly and effectively in public. But the elocution lessons did not help him overcome his shyness. He kept careful records of the money he spent, and he soon decided to cut his expenses and live more frugally. To save money on bus fare, he walked nearly everywhere he went, sometimes as much as 10 miles (16 kilometers) a day. He began to make friends, both Indians and non-Indians, when he became active in the local Vegetarian Society.

Gandhi passed his bar examinations on June 10, 1891. He sailed for India two days later. Upon Gandhi's arrival at the dock in Bombay, his brother Laxmidas delivered the sad news that their mother had died while Gandhi was in England. The family had thought it best to keep this news from him until he returned from England.

Gandhi decided to practice law in Bombay. However, the first time he tried to present a case in court, he was too frightened to speak. He gave his client her money back and told her to find another lawyer. Gandhi then returned to Rajkot, where he handled legal paperwork for Laxmidas and other lawyers but stayed out of the courtrooms. In the course of his business, an encounter with a British officer who treated him rudely left Gandhi disillusioned about his prospects for career advancement in India.

Early in 1893, as Gandhi was pondering his future, a Muslim firm of shipowners and traders from Porbandar offered him a job pursuing a legal claim on its behalf in South Africa. Gandhi accepted the offer. This law assignment was expected to last no more than one year. Gandhi arranged for his wife and children to remain in Rajkot with Laxmidas's family. Their living expenses would be paid by the fee he would receive for the job. Gandhi's second son, Manilal, had been born on Oct. 28, 1892. Gandhi set sail on April 19, 1893, and arrived in Durban on May 23. In 1893, South Africa, like India, was partly under British control. Durban was the capital of Natal, one of four British *crown colonies* (a colony under the control and authority of the British crown that came under British control after the Anglo-Boer War that ended in 1902). The other three were the Cape Colony, the Transvaal, and the Orange Free State. Before the war, the British had fought the Afrikaners for control of the colonies.

Almost immediately, Gandhi was abused because he was an Indian who claimed his rights as a British subject. During a train ride from Durban to Pretoria on the bitterly cold night of June 7, 1893—June is a winter month in the Southern Hemisphere—a white passenger objected to sharing a first-class compartment with Gandhi. Railway officials asked Gandhi to move to the third-class section at the back of the train, which was reserved for "Coloured" people. But Gandhi showed them his first-class ticket and refused to get out. He was removed from the train by a constable and spent the rest of the night without his overcoat in a dark, chilly waiting room at the station in Maritzburg.

As he sat shivering, Gandhi pondered his situation and reached a turning point:

> *I began to think of my duty. Should I fight for my rights or go back to India, or should I go on to Pretoria without minding the insults, and return to India after finishing the case? It would be cowardice to run back to India without fulfilling my obligation. The hardship to which I was subjected was superficial—only a symptom of the deep disease of colour prejudice. I should try, if possible, to root out the disease and suffer hardships in the process. Redress for wrongs I should seek only to the extent that would be necessary for the removal of the colour prejudice. So I decided to take the next available train to Pretoria.*[3]

Gandhi quickly discovered that the Indian population of South Africa was divided into several groups, all of whom suffered from discrimination. Among the free Indians were various professionals, merchants, traders, clerks, and artisans of Hindu, Muslim, and Parsi faiths. But the largest group by far was composed of low-paid indentured laborers and their families, who had been coming to Natal from northern India since 1860. These laborers arrived on a five-year contract to work on farms. Many of them chose to become permanent residents, either by renewing their labor contract or by settling as free workers on land given to them by the government in place of their return passage. These unskilled laborers were known as "coolies," a term the British insultingly applied to other Indians as well.

In the spring of 1894, Gandhi brought to a successful close the business for which he had been sent to South Africa. He had been able to persuade the arguing parties to avoid a costly court battle by settling their differences through arbitration. At the urging of fellow Indians in Natal, Gandhi decided to stay in South Africa a bit longer to work for Indian rights. Little did he know then that he would remain for 20 more years.

## THE SEARCH FOR TRUTH, THE PRINCIPLE OF NONVIOLENCE

Gandhi established a private law practice in order to support himself financially while doing free public work in South Africa. His immediate concern in 1894 was to organize opposition to a bill that would deny all Indians the right to vote for representatives to the Natal Legislative Assembly. At the time, eligibility to vote was based on wealth rather than ancestry, and about 250 Indians met the wealth requirement. The bill passed, but Gandhi attracted considerable attention for the issue of Indian rights by organizing a huge group of volunteers who in only two weeks collected the signatures of about 10,000 Indians throughout Natal on a "monster petition" that was presented to the secretary of state for the colonies. Outside of South Africa, both the *Times of India* and the London *Times* supported the petition. With Gandhi's guidance, the Natal Indian Congress was formed on May 22, 1894, to lead the campaign for Indian rights in South Africa.

*Gandhi,* center, *is surrounded by workers in his law office at Johannesburg, South Africa, in 1902. Gandhi, the country's first person of color to be admitted to the bar, spent most of his 20 years in South Africa protesting the treatment of Indians by the British.*

Throughout his time in South Africa, Gandhi continued to be an avid reader in his search for truth. The work of the Russian writer Leo Tolstoy made a lasting impression on him. Although today best known for his masterpiece novels *War and Peace* (1869) and *Anna Karenina* (1875–1877), Tolstoy also was an important moral and religious thinker and social reformer. In his essay "The Kingdom of God Is Within You" (1894), Tolstoy explained his belief that people are able to know and affirm the good in themselves if they engage in self-examination and willingly reform themselves. He also believed that any use of violence or force is harmful and that opposition to force should be expressed nonviolently. These ideas affirmed Gandhi's principles of truth-seeking and nonviolence.

By 1896, Gandhi realized he would be in for a long stay in South Africa. He decided to return to India to get his wife and children and bring them back to Natal with him. He also hoped to sway public opinion in India in support of the Indians' struggle in South Africa. He sailed for India on June 5, 1896.

While in Rajkot with his family, Gandhi wrote a pamphlet titled *The Grievances of the British Indians in South Africa*. It had a green cover and thus became known more commonly as the Green Pamphlet. Ten thousand copies were printed and distributed to newspapers and leaders of India's numerous political parties. With the promise of his blessing and the offer of some used postage stamps he had collected, Gandhi recruited schoolchildren as volunteers in their spare time to wrap the pamphlets for the mail. The Green Pamphlet detailed the abuses to which Indians in South Africa were subjected—ranging from being called names and spat upon on the street to being refused entry into tramcars, hotels, and public baths—and argued that the Indians were being denied their rights as British subjects. This argument was based on a royal proclamation of 1858 that declared Indians were equal citizens of the British Empire. Gandhi, who cherished his loyalty to the British constitution, believed that South Africa's color prejudice was "quite contrary to British traditions" and would therefore be "only temporary and local"[4] until these injustices were brought to light and rectified.

Gandhi sailed from Bombay on Nov. 30, 1896, taking with him his wife and two sons and his widowed sister's only son, who was 10 years old. Upon arrival in Durban, all ships from Bombay were quarantined for about five days and inspected by the local medical officer to make sure they were free of the plague that had broken out in Bombay earlier that year. But Gandhi's ship was detained longer than that. The medical officer who was about to give the ship a clean bill of health was suddenly replaced. The new medical officer called for an additional quarantine of 11 days and ordered the passengers to burn or disinfect all their clothes. Passenger quarters were fumigated. Food and water began to run out, but no fresh provisions were allowed in. Soon Gandhi discovered the real reason for the delay. The white ruling elite of Natal had found out about the Green Pamphlet and objected to its contents as "unmerited condemnation." Furthermore, the group believed that Gandhi had brought the passengers of his ship and another from Bombay "with a view to swamping Natal with Indians."[5] Gandhi insisted that his family members were the only passengers he knew and that everyone aboard had the right to land at Port Natal. He also refuted the charge regarding the Green Pamphlet, noting that he said nothing in it that he had not already said before leaving Natal and that he had ample evidence to support his claims. The passengers finally were allowed to disembark on Jan. 13, 1897.

The Gandhi family settled in a large house in Durban. They called the house Beach Grove Villas. The children wore Western-style clothes and were instructed by an English governess. Gandhi's two younger sons were born in 1897 and 1900. Gandhi himself delivered his fourth son when Kasturbai's labor progressed too fast for a doctor to arrive in time.

Gandhi led many campaigns for Indian rights in South Africa, but he also worked for the British when he felt justice was on their side.

He was decorated by the British for paramedic work in the Anglo-Boer War of 1899–1902. This war was the second and longer of two struggles between the British and the *Boers*—white descendants of Dutch farmers who arrived in the mid-1600's (now called Afrikaners). An earlier war was fought from 1880 to 1881. The wars involved the Boers of the northern South African regions of the Orange Free State and the South African Republic (also called Transvaal). The main cause of the wars was the United Kingdom's desire for supremacy in South Africa.

Although Gandhi continued to publish pamphlets and brochures and to write to newspapers in South Africa, India, and England, he felt that there should be an independent newspaper to serve the needs of the Indian community. He helped start the weekly newspaper *Indian Opinion*, which began publication on June 4, 1903. The following year, Gandhi bought the newspaper and the press it was printed on. He published the paper in English and Gujarati.

In October 1904, during a long, overnight train ride into Durban, Gandhi read *Unto This Last* (1862), a collection of four essays on social issues written by the influential English critic John Ruskin. Ruskin questioned the operations and motives of the free enterprise system, and he urged workers to express their individuality. Gandhi understood Ruskin to be saying that all work has equal value and that a life of farming and making goods by hand was the life worth living. "I believe that I discovered some of my deepest convictions reflected in this great book of Ruskin," Gandhi recalled in his autobiography, "and that is why it so captured me and made me transform my life."[6]

## THE DEVELOPMENT OF SATYAGRAHA

When Gandhi returned home, he and his business partner Albert West bought an estate called Phoenix about 14 miles (22 kilometers) from Durban. Situated on about 100 acres (40 hectares) of land, the property featured "a dilapidated cottage,"[7] a small spring, and some orange and mango trees. With help from fellow Anglo-Boer War veterans, Gandhi constructed a large building out of wood and corrugated iron to house his printing press. Then he and a group of relatives and friends—both Indian and

European—established a cooperative farming community based on a Hindu *ashram* (a small rural retreat for meditation). Gandhi divided his time between Phoenix and his law office in Johannesburg. He also kept his family home, Beach Grove Villas, but greatly simplified the lifestyle maintained there. After much deliberation, Gandhi in 1906 took the vow of *brahmacharya* (celibacy) and adopted a blander, simpler diet with periodic fasting. He took these actions in order to exert greater self-control over his body and focus his energy toward his ongoing search for truth.

The British gave colonial self-government to the Transvaal in 1907. The Boers quickly gained control. On March 22, 1907, the Transvaal Parliament passed the Asiatic Registration Act. This new law required that all Indians register with the government by July 31 and receive a *permit,* or certificate of registration. After this deadline, police officers could at any time stop any Indian, anywhere—even on the street or in a private home—and demand to see the permit. Failure to register or to produce the required permit was punishable by fine, imprisonment, or even deportation. Gandhi and his followers, dubbing this racially discriminatory law the Black Act, formed the Passive Resistance Association, and refused to register. In fact, only about 5 percent of the Indian population had registered by July 31. As a result of such widespread noncompliance, the deadline was extended a number of times.

As the struggle for Indian rights continued, Gandhi decided that the term *passive resistance* was inadequate to describe his method of direct social action based on principles of courage, nonviolence, and truth. He eventually came up with the term *Satyagraha,* explaining, "Truth (*satya*) implies love, and firmness (*agraha*) engenders and therefore serves as a synonym for force."[8] In another writing, he added, "Satyagraha is literally holding on to Truth and it means, therefore, Truth-force. Truth is soul or spirit. It is, therefore, known as soul-force. It excludes the use of violence because man is not capable of knowing the absolute truth and, therefore, not competent to punish."[9]

From 1907 to 1914, the practice of Satyagraha in South Africa took various forms, including picketing permit offices, burning registration certificates, and crossing borders illegally. On Jan. 11, 1908, Gandhi and other Indians who had refused to register were brought before a judge. They pleaded guilty and were sentenced to prison. Gandhi was locked in a cell in the courtroom and then driven to Johannesburg Jail, where he remained imprisoned for about two months. During that time, he read a number of sacred and philosophical works, including the essay "Civil Disobedience" (1849) by the American writer Henry David Thoreau. In this work, Thoreau said that people should refuse to obey any law they believe is unjust. Gandhi picked up on the phrase *civil disobedience* as a term that might be more familiar to English readers than *Satyagraha* and used it on occasion to help them better understand the struggles he was trying to explain. Gandhi, his wife, and many of his followers were jailed several more times during this Satyagraha campaign.

In 1910, Gandhi established a second cooperative community near Johannesburg. He named it Tolstoy Farm after the Russian writer, with whom he corresponded in 1909 and 1910. Gandhi abandoned Western dress in favor of the *dhoti,* a traditional Indian garment made of a piece of white cloth wrapped around the waist and between the legs. Increasingly large numbers of people called Gandhi *Bapu* (father) and joined him in marches, strikes, and other peaceful protest activities. In 1914, Gandhi's efforts resulted in victory when the British abolished their punitive tax on former indentured laborers and gave legal recognition to Hindu, Muslim, and Parsi marriages. He then decided to return to his homeland to work for Indian independence from the British. He had already formulated some of his plans in his 80-page book *Hind Swaraj* (*Indian Home Rule*), which he had written in 1909 and published in installments in *Indian Opinion.*

## CAMPAIGNS FOR INDIAN INDEPENDENCE

Gandhi and his wife sailed from Durban on July 18, 1914. They decided to make a stop in England before returning to India. Two days before they arrived, World War I (1914–1918) broke out. Gandhi organized a volunteer ambulance corps of about 80 Indians, most of them students in the United

Kingdom, to help the British in the war effort. When Gandhi and his wife finally reached India on Jan. 9, 1915, they were welcomed at the dock by a large crowd. On May 25, 1915, Gandhi founded the Satyagraha Ashram at Sabarmati, on a tract of land across the Sabarmati River from the city of Ahmedabad in Bombay Presidency (a former administrative division of British India). There he lived a simple lifestyle with about two dozen family members and followers. Within five years, Gandhi became the leader of the Indian nationalist movement.

In 1919, the British imperial government introduced the Rowlatt bills to make it unlawful to organize opposition to the government. Gandhi led a Satyagraha campaign that succeeded in preventing passage of one of these two bills. The other was never enforced. Gandhi called off the campaign when riots broke out. He then fasted to impress the people with the need to be nonviolent. Also in 1919, Gandhi took charge of two Indian newspapers, the English-language *Young India* and the Gujarati *Navajivan,* which he published weekly from his own press in Ahmedabad.

The cruelty of imperial rule was demonstrated in Amritsar, an Indian city in the northern Punjab state, on April 13, 1919. That day, tens of thousands of Indians assembled in an enclosed area called the Jallianwala Bagh. As a political speaker began to address the gathering, British troops entered the meeting place and blocked the entrance. General R. E. H. Dyer, the British commander, mustered 50 soldiers with rifles, got them into position, and—without warning the crowd to disperse—ordered the soldiers to open fire on the unarmed crowd and keep shooting until they ran out of ammunition. The trapped people desperately scrambled to escape. The shots killed about 400 people and wounded about 1,200. Dyer declared martial law and imposed such tight censorship on the community that it took weeks for news of the massacre to reach the rest of India. Several months later, a committee of inquiry ruled that Dyer acted beyond the needs of the situation and with little humanity, and he was relieved of his command. The Amritsar Massacre was a turning point for India. From then on, Indians lost faith in British justice and demanded complete independence from British rule.

In response, the British promised reforms. However, at the same time, they tried to crush the independence movement.

## NONVIOLENT DISOBEDIENCE

In the aftermath of the Amritsar Massacre, Gandhi became even more determined to develop Satyagraha and to win India's independence through nonviolent resistance. By 1920, Gandhi had become a leader in the Indian National Congress, which had become the most important Indian political organization. He persuaded the congress to adopt his program of *nonviolent disobedience*, also known as *nonviolent noncooperation*. Under this program, Indians were asked to boycott British goods, to refuse to pay taxes, and to stop using British schools, courts, and government services. Some Indians who followed the program gave up jobs that paid well but required them to cooperate with the British. Gandhi changed the Indian National Congress from a small party of educated men to a party of the people with millions of men, women, and children as followers.

Also about 1920, Gandhi began a program of hand spinning and weaving. He believed that making one's own *khadi* (coarse, hand-loomed, white cotton cloth) and clothing would promote economic, social, and political freedom for India. The program would aid economic freedom by making India self-sufficient in cloth. It would encourage social freedom through the dignity of labor. It would advance political freedom by challenging the British textile industry and by preparing Indians for self-government. Gandhi envisioned an independent India with a political system based on self-governing groups of villages rather than a Western-style central government.

Gandhi led three major Satyagraha campaigns in India: from 1920 to 1922, from 1930 to 1934, and from 1940 to 1942. He spent time in prison during each one. Altogether, he spent seven years in prison for political activity. He believed that it is honorable to go to jail for a good cause. He also fasted a number of times for various reasons—for example, to show support for striking workers, to protest the lack of rights for untouchables, or to stop Hindus and Muslims from fighting.

*Indians in Delhi participate in a foreign cloth boycott on July 26, 1922. A leader in the Indian National Congress, Gandhi persuaded the congress to adopt his program of nonviolent disobedience. Under this program, Indians were asked to boycott British goods, to refuse to pay taxes, and to stop using British schools, courts, and government services.*

Gandhi brought the nonviolent tactic of the protest march into greater prominence in 1930. On March 12, Gandhi and 78 followers began a 24-day march from Satyagraha Ashram through the villages of Gujarat to the seacoast at Dandi, about 240 miles (386 kilometers) away. Others joined the march along the way. By the time the procession reached the sea, it included thousands of people. When they arrived, Gandhi made salt from seawater. This action was a protest against the Salt Acts, which made it a crime to possess salt not bought from the British government. The government taxed the salt it sold, and Gandhi found this tax on such a basic commodity unjust. British authorities did not arrest Gandhi immediately but finally imprisoned him about a month later, on May 5. The march, which came to be known as the salt march or the Dandi march, aroused enormous public interest. More than 60,000 people followed Gandhi's example during 1930 by making salt and going to prison.

The salt march and other acts of civil disobedience in the 1930's led the British to give the Indian people more political power. In 1931, Gandhi and the British viceroy of India, Lord Irwin, signed an agreement in which Gandhi would give up his campaign of civil

*In 1930, Gandhi, fourth from left, led followers on a 240-mile (386-kilometer) march from Satyagraha Ashram through the villages of Gujarat to the seacoast at Dandi, where Gandhi made salt from seawater. This was a protest against the Salt Acts, which made it a crime to possess salt not bought from the government.*

disobedience and the British would release thousands of political prisoners. The Government of India Act of 1935 created a new constitution that increased the representation of Indians in all branches of government and gave local legislatures more control in the provinces. However, the British government retained control over finances and kept its veto power. Thus, even under the new constitution, the Indians did not get many of the changes they wanted.

During World War II (1939–1945), Gandhi continued his struggle for India's freedom through campaigns of nonviolent disobedience to British rule. Gandhi wanted one country for all Indians, and he urged Hindus and Muslims to live together in peace. However, in 1940, the leader of the Muslim League, Mohammad Ali Jinnah, demanded that a new country for Muslims be carved out of India. The Muslim League cooperated with the British during the war with the understanding that its demand would receive serious consideration.

## INDIA'S INDEPENDENCE

Early in 1946, the British declared that they would grant India independence if Indian political leaders could agree on a form of government, but the Indian National Congress and the

Muslim League could not settle their differences. Violent clashes between Muslims and Hindus broke out. To end the violence, Indian and British leaders in 1947 agreed to *partition* (divide) the country. On August 14, the independent nation of Pakistan was formed. It consisted of two parts, West Pakistan and East Pakistan, carved out of the northwestern and northeastern parts of India and separated by more than 1,000 miles (1,609 kilometers) of Indian territory. India became an independent nation on August 15.

But the partition was accompanied by more violence and bloodshed. More than 10 million people became refugees, as Hindus and Sikhs in Pakistan fled to India, and Muslims in India fled to Pakistan. About half a million people were killed in Hindu-Muslim riots. On Jan. 13, 1948, at the age of 78, Gandhi began a fast to end the bloodshed among Hindu, Muslim, and other groups. On January 18, their leaders pledged to stop fighting, and Gandhi broke his fast.

## ASSASSINATION AND LEGACY

Late in the afternoon of Jan. 30, 1948, Gandhi made his way to a prayer meeting in New Delhi. As he walked through the crowd, his palms pressed together in the traditional Hindu greeting, a man rushed forward and shot him three times at pointblank range. "He Ram" ("Oh God"), Gandhi murmured as he sank to the ground and died. The assassin, Nathuram Godse, was a Hindu fanatic who opposed Gandhi's program of tolerance. The next day, thousands of mourners lined the streets of Gandhi's funeral procession. As Gandhi had requested, his body was not preserved, and it was cremated in accordance with Hindu custom on the banks of the Jumna River. His ashes later were scattered in the river. Godse was convicted of murder and hanged on Nov. 15, 1949.

Gandhi's influence far outlasted his life. The Indian Constitution of 1950 outlawed untouchability and gave untouchables full citizenship. Gandhi's principles of nonviolent resistance have been successfully implemented in many parts of the world to gain freedom or bring about social justice. ■

# Chronology of King's Life

1929    born on January 15, in Atlanta, Georgia

1948    ordained minister at Ebenezer Baptist Church in Atlanta; receives bachelor of arts degree in sociology from Morehouse College in Atlanta

1951    receives bachelor of divinity degree from Crozer Theology Seminary in Chester, Pennsylvania

1953    marries Coretta Scott on June 18 in Marion, Alabama

1954    takes pastorate position at Dexter Avenue Baptist Church in Montgomery, Alabama

1955    receives doctorate in systematic theology from Boston University School of Theology; helps organize protest of Montgomery's segregated bus system

1956    U.S. Supreme Court orders Montgomery to provide equal, integrated seating on public buses

1957    with other black ministers, founds the Southern Christian Leadership Conference (SCLC) to expand the nonviolent struggle against racism and discrimination

1960    moves from Montgomery to Atlanta to devote more effort to SCLC's work; with his father, becomes co-pastor of Ebenezer Baptist Church

1963    with SCLC associates, launches massive demonstrations to protest racial discrimination in Birmingham, Alabama; with other civil rights leaders, organizes the massive March on Washington, D.C., on Aug. 28 to highlight African American unemployment and to urge Congress to pass President John F. Kennedy's civil rights bill; King delivers famous "I Have a Dream" speech at March on Washington

1964    Congress approves Civil Rights Act of 1964; King receives Nobel Peace Prize for leading nonviolent civil rights demonstration

1965    helps organize protests in Selma, Alabama, where black citizens are denied  the chance to register and vote; Congress approves Voting Rights Act of 1965

1966    helps begin major civil rights campaign in Chicago to organize black inner-city residents suffering from unemployment, bad housing, and poor schools

1967    begins to plan Poor People's Campaign to unite poor people of all races in a struggle for economic opportunity

1968    shot and killed by James Earl Ray on April 4 in Memphis

# Martin Luther King, Jr. (1929–1968)

Martin Luther King, Jr., was the foremost leader of the American civil rights movement in the 1950's and 1960's. A gifted orator, King first developed his passionate speaking style as a Baptist minister and later refined it as an internationally famous spokesperson for social justice. Under King's leadership, the civil rights movement accomplished the legal abolishment of racial segregation in the South and inspired passage of such important national legislation as the Civil Rights Act of 1964 and the Voting Rights Act of 1965.

King's steadfast philosophy of nonviolence echoed that of the great Indian leader Mohandas K. Gandhi. Although King and Gandhi never met, Gandhi once predicted that it "may be through the Negroes that the unadulterated message of Non-violence will be delivered to the world."[1] King bore out that prediction. Like Gandhi before him, King's philosophy of nonviolence was rooted in his deeply felt sense

*King's abiding faith in Christian love made him view racial equality as a moral imperative for the spiritual well-being of all people. King, left, and Ralph Abernathy,* center back, *kneel with a group in prayer prior to going to jail in Selma, Alabama, on Feb. 10, 1965. The group was arrested on February 1st, after attempting to gain the right to vote.*

of spirituality. In King's case, it was his abiding faith in Christian love that made him view racial equality as a moral imperative for the spiritual well-being of all people. Like Gandhi, King did not have an imposing physical presence—King's adult height was only about 5 feet, 7 inches—but his charismatic presence and resonant voice drew people to him. In his personal life, and in his stirring speeches, King always tried to bring forth something positive from even the worst experiences. It was a cruel irony for a preacher of peace that, like Gandhi, King was shot to death by an assassin.

# Chapter 1: Early Life

## CHILDHOOD

Martin Luther King, Jr., was born on Jan. 15, 1929, in Atlanta, Georgia. A doctor helped deliver him at the family home, a large Victorian-style house at 501 Auburn Avenue. At birth, King was so quiet that the doctor, fearing the baby might be stillborn, spanked him several times until he cried to confirm his new life. The child was first named Michael King, Jr., after his father, Michael King. He grew up at the house on Auburn Avenue, where he lived with his father; his mother, Alberta Williams King; an older sister, Christine, born in 1927; a younger brother, Alfred Daniel, called A. D., born in 1930; and his mother's parents, Adam Daniel Williams and Jennie Celeste Williams, whom the children called Mama.

King's grandfather Williams was pastor of the Ebenezer Baptist Church, about one block from the King home. King's father served as assistant pastor. On March 21, 1931, the Reverend Williams died of a heart attack, and the elder King became pastor. In 1934, at the request of his own dying father, the elder King changed both his name and his son's name from Michael to Martin Luther. The boy was usually called M. L. Also in 1934, at the age of 5, M. L. became an official member of Ebenezer Baptist after a guest evangelist invited the children in the Sunday school class to join the church. As King recalled in his autobiography, "My sister was the first one to join the church that morning, and after seeing her join I decided that I would not let her get ahead of me, so I was the next. I had never given this matter a thought, and even at the time of my baptism I was unaware of what was taking place. From this it seems quite clear that I joined the church not out of any dynamic conviction, but out of a childhood desire to keep up with my sister."[1] However, King considered the church a "second home" and credited his Sunday school classes for helping him learn how to get along with people.

Young M. L. was a bit small for his age but nonetheless a healthy, happy child. His parents were loving but strict. When the children

*King was born Jan. 15, 1929, at his family's large Victorian-style home at 501 Auburn Avenue, in Atlanta. In 1980, an area including King's birthplace, church, and burial place became the Martin Luther King, Jr., National Historic Site.*

misbehaved, their father whipped their backsides with a strap, a punishment fairly common in the United States at that time. But Daddy King—as young M. L. called him—also praised his children when they did well at their tasks, and he gave them a weekly allowance for ice cream and soft drinks. The family's social life revolved mainly around the church, where hearty Sunday dinners included ham, fried chicken, black-eyed peas, and watermelon.

M. L.'s closest friend in the neighborhood was a white boy whose father owned a store across the street from the King house. The boys played together from the age of about 3 until they entered kindergarten in September 1935—at separate schools. Soon afterward, M. L.'s friend told him that they could not play together anymore because the friend's father had forbidden it. M. L. was shocked and confused. He discussed the situation with his parents at the dinner table and, for the first time, he became aware of the racism that existed in American society.

At the time King was born, Alabama and other states in the South followed a policy of *segregation*—that is, legal separation of people by race. The idea behind segregation in the United States—that white people were considered superior to black people and therefore the two groups should not mix—dated back several hundred years. From the 1600's until the American Civil War (1861–1865), blacks were shipped across the Atlantic Ocean from western Africa against their will. Most worked as slaves throughout the South. In December 1865, the adoption of the 13th Amendment to the U.S. Constitution officially ended slavery throughout the nation. But racial discrimination continued, especially in the South.

In the late 1800's, many Southern states adopted *Jim Crow laws* requiring that blacks and whites use separate public facilities. The term *Jim Crow* originally referred to a black character in a popular song from the 1830's. A series of decisions by the Supreme Court of the United States supported the rapid spread of Jim Crow laws through the South. The most influential of these decisions was *Plessy v. Ferguson.* In this 1896 landmark case, the Supreme Court upheld a Louisiana law that required "separate but equal" facilities for blacks and whites in railroad cars. The plaintiff, Homer A. Plessy, had argued that the defendant, the criminal court district judge John H. Ferguson, erred in overruling Plessy's original plea that the Louisiana law violated a clause of the 14th Amendment to the U.S. Constitution that guaranteed citizens equal protection under the law. The Supreme Court ruled that the amendment did not seek to guarantee the social equality of all races. Thus, segregation of the races in the South continued. Many states used the "separate but equal" rule to segregate black children in public schools and black citizens in transportation, recreation, sleeping, and eating facilities. The separate facilities for blacks, who were referred to as "colored" or "Negroes," were nearly always inferior to those for whites.

During King's childhood, "Whites only" signs in Atlanta blocked his access to city parks, public swimming pools, downtown lunch counters, the YMCA, and most movie theaters. One day at a shoe store with his father, a white clerk asked the two of them to take seats in the back of the store to be waited on. Seats in the front were reserved for white customers. Daddy King refused to move, grasped his son's hand, and walked out of the store, furiously muttering, "I don't care how long I have to live with this system, I will never accept it."[2] Another time, after M. L. had wandered away from his mother while shopping in a downtown store, a white woman suddenly slapped him for no apparent reason and insultingly called him a "nigger." He did not strike back, but he later told his mother what had happened, and they left the store. Such indignities fostered in young M. L. a sense of hatred against white people. However, his parents told him that it was his duty as a Christian to love all people, even white people. Yet the question lingered in the boy's mind: "How could I love a race of people who hated me?"[3]

In addition to such social discrimination based on race, black Americans in the early 1930's also faced job discrimination as a result of the Great Depression, a worldwide economic slump. By 1933, the national unemployment rate had reached a staggering 25 percent overall, but unemployment rates among blacks were much higher than those for whites. Many jobless people and their families had to depend on the government or charity to provide them with food. King remembered, as a young child, seeing people standing in bread lines. Unemployment did not substantially decline until 1942, after the United States had entered World War II (1939–1945).

King attended Yonge Street Elementary School from kindergarten through fifth grade. His subjects included math, history, and grammar. Schoolwork was easy for him. On the afternoon of May 18, 1941, M. L. sneaked away from his studies at home to watch a parade. His enjoyment of the parade was interrupted by a messenger who told him something had happened to his grandmother. M. L. rushed home and discovered to his dismay that his beloved Mama had suffered a heart attack and had died on the way to the hospital. Overcome with grief and a sense of guilt that God was punishing him for running off to the parade by taking Mama away from him, M. L. ran upstairs and jumped out a window, hoping to follow her in death. But it was not his time to go. The bruises left on his body did not hurt as badly as the pain he felt inside over the loss of his grandmother, who had been a nurturing presence in the household. After her death, M. L. had a lengthy discussion with his parents about the Christian *doctrine* (accepted teaching) of immortality, which explains that a person's soul continues to exist even after the death of the body. M. L. was comforted by the thought that "somehow my grandmother still lived."[4] Soon afterward, the King family moved to a two-story yellow brick house at 193 Boulevard Street, on a bluff overlooking downtown Atlanta. Daddy King was becoming prominent in the city's black community through his leadership role in the Atlanta branch of the National Association for the Advancement of Colored People (NAACP), the Negro Voters League, and other organizations. Daddy King's increased prominence raised the family's social status but also brought on nasty phone calls and hate mail from the Ku Klux Klan (KKK), a white secret society that opposes the advancement of blacks, Jews, and other minority groups.

In sixth grade, M. L. transferred to David T. Howard Colored Elementary School. In the fall of 1942, at the age of 13, he entered Booker T. Washington High School. He especially enjoyed his history

*During King's child-hood, signs marking segregated facilities, like this drinking fountain, were commonplace in the American South.*

and English classes but overall found the schoolwork unchallenging. He did so well in high school that he skipped both the 9th and 12th grades. In his early teens, M. L. struggled with the typical adolescent feelings of rebellion. He channeled much of his aggression into sand-lot baseball, backyard football, and pickup basketball games. He disliked fighting but would settle a dispute with a peer by wrestling if negotiation failed. Unwilling to confront his powerful father directly, M. L. defied him in subtle ways, such as challenging the teachings in his Sunday school classes. As his voice deepened into a hearty baritone, M. L. discovered that it attracted people's attention. Some of this attention came from girls, and M. L. began to take greater notice of them in return. He took to wearing stylish tweed suits that earned him the nickname "Tweedie." M. L. liked to dance the jitterbug with pretty young women. He also played the violin and developed a taste for opera. In quieter moments, M. L. shut himself up in his room and read the works of orators whom he admired for their "eloquent statement of ideas."[5]

On April 17, 1944, when he was in the 11th grade, King traveled by bus with a favorite teacher, Mrs. Bradley, to participate in an oratory contest in Dublin, Georgia. King won the contest with his powerful presentation of his speech "The Negro and the Constitution," which was later reprinted in his autobiography:

> We cannot have an enlightened democracy with one great group living in ignorance. We cannot have a healthy nation with one-tenth of the people ill-nourished, sick, harboring germs of disease which recognize no color lines—obey no Jim Crow laws. We cannot have a nation orderly and sound with one group so ground down and thwarted that it is almost forced into unsocial attitudes and crime. We cannot be truly Christian people so long as we flout the central teachings of Jesus: brotherly love and the Golden Rule. We cannot come to full prosperity with one great group so ill-delayed that it cannot buy goods. So as we gird ourselves to defend democracy from foreign attack, let us see to it that increasingly at home we give fair play and free opportunity for all people.
>
> Today 13 million black sons and daughters of our forefathers continue the fight for the translation of the 13th, 14th, and 15th Amendments from writing on the printed page to an actuality. We believe with them that "if freedom is good for any it is good for all," that we may conquer Southern armies by the sword, but it is another thing to conquer Southern hate, that if the franchise is given to Negroes, they will be vigilant and defend, even with their arms, the ark of federal liberty from treason and destruction by her enemies.[6]

On the ride home from the contest, the bus was full. Along the way, some white passengers got on, and the white bus driver ordered King and his black teacher to give up their seats to the new arrivals. "We didn't move quickly enough to suit him," King recalled, "so he began cursing us. I intended to stay right in that seat, but Mrs. Bradley urged me up, saying we had to obey the law. We stood up in the aisle for 90 miles [144 kilometers] to Atlanta. That night will never leave my memory. It was the angriest I have ever been in my life."[7]

Later in the spring of 1944, at the age of 15, King passed the entrance exam for Morehouse College in Atlanta. He graduated from Booker T. Washington High School and made plans to enter Morehouse in the fall. King spent the summer of 1944 working on a tobacco farm in Simsbury, Connecticut, to earn extra money for college. In a letter to his father dated June 15, King wrote, "On our way here we saw some things I had never anticipated to see. After we passed Washington there was no discrimination at all[;] the white people here are very nice. We go to any place we want to and sit any where we want to."[8] He even dined in one of the finest restaurants in nearby Hartford without any problems. In his autobiography, King recalled the bitterness he felt about returning to the segregated South at the end of that summer: "It was hard to understand why I could ride wherever I pleased on the train from New York to Washington and then had to change to a Jim Crow car at the nation's capital in order to continue the trip to Atlanta. The first time that I was seated behind a curtain in a dining car [to be segregated from the white diners], I felt as if the curtain had been dropped on my self-hood. I could never adjust to the separate waiting rooms, separate eating places, separate rest rooms, partly because the separate was always unequal, and partly because the very idea of separation did something to my sense of dignity and self-respect."[9]

## HIGHER EDUCATION

On Sept. 20, 1944, the 15-year-old Martin Luther King, Jr., started his freshman year at Morehouse College in Atlanta—the college both his father and his maternal grandfather had attended. In the younger King's day, the school had only a few hundred students and allowed only men. Spelman College for women was nearby. King was appalled to discover that the reading skills he had acquired as an excellent student at the "colored" schools did not measure up to the demands of college courses, but he quickly made up for that deficiency. He declared a major in sociology and considered eventually becoming a lawyer or a doctor to satisfy his "deep urge to serve humanity."[10] King joined the glee club and the football team to become more active in campus life. But his most important extracurricular activity was his participation in the Intercollegiate Council, where for the first time he met white students who shared his concern for racial and economic justice. As a result of this experience, his resentment against white people began to ease up and become replaced by a new spirit of cooperation.

While he was at Morehouse, King read the essay "Civil Disobedience" (1849) by the American writer Henry David Thoreau for the first time. In it, Thoreau argued that people should refuse to obey any law they believe is unjust. Thoreau had put his belief into practice in 1846 when he refused to pay poll taxes in protest over his opposition to slavery, as it became an issue in the Mexican War (1846–1848). Thoreau spent a night in jail for his refusal. In Thoreau's essay, King recalled, "I made my first contact with the theory of nonviolent resistance. Fascinated by the idea of refusing to cooperate with an evil system, I was so deeply moved that I reread the work several times. I became convinced that noncooperation with evil is as much a moral obligation as is cooperation with good."[11]

During the summers of his college years, King worked as a manual laborer unloading trains and trucks so that he could gain a better understanding of what life was like for people who were of lower socioeconomic status and who held such jobs permanently. He soon noticed that the black laborers got paid less than the white laborers did for doing the same work and were treated more disrespectfully. This experience reinforced the teachings of his sociology adviser, Walter Chivers, who said that *capitalism*—that is, an economic system in which privately owned businesses determine how resources will be used, what mix of goods and services will be provided, and how goods and services will be distributed among the members of society—exploited black people and encouraged racism. King wrote a letter to the editor of the *Atlanta Constitution* that was published on Aug. 6, 1946, condemning the ill treatment of "the Negro." He concluded, "We want and are entitled to the basic rights and opportunities of American citizens: The right to earn a living at work for which we are fitted by training and ability; equal opportunities in education, health, recreation, and similar public services; the right to vote; equality before the law; some of the same courtesy and good manners that we ourselves bring to all human relations."[12]

King's feelings toward religion changed during his years at Morehouse, largely due to the influence of university president Benjamin E. Mays and religion professor George D. Kelsey. Both men were ministers as well as scholars, and they helped King reconcile his skepticism concerning "whether religion could be intellectually respectable as well as emotionally satisfying."[13] Kelsey's course on the Bible helped King "see that behind the legends and myths of the Book were many profound truths which one could not escape."[14] King also realized that in black communities in the South, the local preacher often served as a powerful political leader as well as a spiritual leader. Thus, the pulpit could become a platform for social justice. King's father was overjoyed at his son's choice to enter the ministry. The younger King was ordained on Feb. 25, 1948, at the age of 18, at Ebenezer Baptist Church. He received a bachelor of arts degree in sociology from Morehouse College on June 8, 1948.

On Sept. 14, 1948, King entered Crozer Theological Seminary, a small, private, nondenominational school in Chester, Pennsylvania. There he embarked on "a serious intellectual quest for a method to eliminate social evil," examining "the social and ethical theories of the great philosophers, from Plato and Aristotle down to Rousseau, Hobbes, Bentham, Mill, and Locke."[15] Plato and his pupil Aristotle were ancient Greek philosophers. Jean-Jacques Rousseau was a French philosopher whose ideas helped shape the political events that led to the French Revolution (1789–1799). Thomas Hobbes was a British philosopher and political theorist. The British philosopher Jeremy Bentham developed a philosophy called Utilitarianism, which included the idea that a person should always do what will produce the greatest good for the greatest number of people. The British writer and utilitarian philosopher John Stuart Mill modified and expanded upon Bentham's principles. John Locke was an English philosopher who believed that the task of a government was to adequately protect its citizens' human rights, including life, political equality, and ownership of property.

King also was impressed by the book *Christianity and the Social Crisis*, written by Walter Rauschenbusch, a theologian who taught at Rochester Theological Seminary in Rochester, New York, in the 1890's and was critical of the capitalist system. King agreed with Rauschenbusch's insistence that the Christian gospel deals with people's material well-being as well as their spiritual well-being. King decided that "any religion that professes concern for the souls of men and is not equally concerned about the slums that damn them, the economic conditions that strangle them, and the social conditions that cripple them is a spiritually moribund religion only waiting for the day to be buried."[16] King thus concluded that his ministry would be "a dual process. On the one hand I must attempt to change the soul of individuals so that their societies may be changed. On the other I must attempt to change the societies so that the individual soul will have a change."[17]

During the Christmas holidays of 1949, King delved into the works of Karl Marx, whose writings helped form a foundation for the political and economic system known as Communism. King wanted to try to understand the appeal of Communism, which calls for government control of the economy. During the Great Depression, many people lost faith in capitalism, and some became interested in Communism as an alternative to that system. King agreed with Marx's argument that workers do not receive full value for their labor under capitalism because the business owners keep the profits. However, King objected to the "political totalitarianism" he saw in Communism. Above all, he rejected Communism's "materialistic interpretation" of history, noting that "Communism, avowedly secularistic and materialistic, has no place for God. This I could never accept, for as a Christian I believe that there is a creative personal power in this universe who is the ground and essence of all reality—a power that cannot be explained in materialistic terms. History is ultimately guided by spirit, not matter."[18]

King continued his philosophical odyssey at Crozer with his first exposure to *pacifism*—that is, a belief system that in its strictest sense opposes war and all other violence, even in self-defense—through a campus lecturer, Dr. A. J. Muste, a Protestant minister and leader in a nonviolent, Christian-based organization called the Fellowship of Reconciliation (FOR). King was dubious of the concept at the time. He also was disturbed by some of the attacks on Christianity expressed in *The Genealogy of Morals* (1887) and other works he read by the German philosopher Friedrich Nietzsche. King began to despair of the power of love in resolving social conflict.

King's despair lifted on a Sunday afternoon in the spring of 1950. That day, he traveled to Philadelphia, Pennsylvania, for a lecture by Dr. Mordecai Johnson, president of Howard University. Johnson had just returned from a trip to India, and his lecture topic was the life and teachings of the Indian leader Mohandas K. Gandhi. King found Johnson's lecture so "profound and electrifying"[19] that he immediately went out and bought some books by and about Gandhi, including Gandhi's *An Autobiography; or, The Story of My Experiments with Truth*. King read with fascination about Gandhi's successful use of a form of pacifism called *nonviolent resistance* or *Satyagraha* (truth-force or soul-force), a method of direct social action based upon principles of courage, nonviolence, and truth. Gandhi organized campaigns of nonviolent disobedience to British laws that he believed were unfair, and in so doing, he helped India win its long struggle for independence from the United Kingdom in 1947. Although Gandhi was a Hindu, King believed that the principle of Satyagraha could be applied to Christian principles as well. King reflected:

> *Gandhi was probably the first person in history to lift the love ethic of Jesus above mere interaction between individuals to a powerful and effective social force on a large scale. Love for Gandhi was a potent instrument for social and collective transformation. It was in this Gandhian emphasis on love and nonviolence that I discovered the method for social reform that I had been seeking.*[20]

During his senior year at Crozer, King began to read the works of Reinhold Niebuhr, an American theologian known for his writings on ethics. Niebuhr was a pacifist, but he abandoned pacifism in the 1930's when the Nazis came to power in Germany, believing that the Nazis were a symbol of an evil greater than the evil of war. King found Niebuhr's criticism of pacifism to be "a serious distortion"[21] of the idea. In his autobiography, King recalled, "My study of Gandhi convinced me that true pacifism is not nonresistance to evil, but nonviolent resistance to evil," noting that "Gandhi resisted evil with as much vigor and power as the violent resister, but he resisted with love instead of hate."[22]

King graduated from Crozer at the top of his class on May 8, 1951, with a bachelor of divinity degree. He won a scholarship to the

*Following in the footsteps of his father and grandfather, King was ordained a minister at Ebenezer Baptist Church, in Atlanta, in 1948. King,* left, *listens to his father, Martin Luther King, Sr.,* right, *preach a sermon at the church in 1964.*

graduate school of his choice, and he chose Boston University. King's father gave him a new green Chevrolet as a graduation present.

King entered the Boston University School of Theology on Sept. 13, 1951. Although Boston did not have Jim Crow laws, racial discrimination did occur there in subtler ways. King at first had difficulty finding a place to live in Boston. When he inquired at properties displaying signs indicating rooms available for rent, he repeatedly was told that the rooms had just been rented. He eventually moved into a four-room apartment in a predominantly black neighborhood with a fellow Morehouse graduate he met in Boston. King eagerly plunged into a rigorous program of coursework that included the history of philosophy, the psychology of religion, a thorough study of the New Testament of the Bible, and a comparative examination of such religions as Judaism, Hinduism, Islam, Buddhism, and Zoroastrianism. King took particular interest in the writings of the influential German philosopher G. W. F. Hegel, who argued that to understand any aspect of human culture, it is necessary to retrace and understand its history. King's analysis of Hegel's historical approach, which became known as Hegel's *dialectic,* helped King see that "growth comes through struggle." King brought his coursework to a close in 1954 with a feeling of "divergent intellectual forces converging into a positive social philosophy. One of the main tenets of this philosophy was the conviction that nonviolent resistance was one of the most potent weapons available to oppressed people in their quest for social justice."[23] He would later translate this philosophy into action. After completing his Ph.D. dissertation, titled "A Comparison of the Conceptions of God in the Thinking of Paul Tillich and Henry Nelson Wieman," King received his doctorate in systematic theology on June 5, 1955. Tillich was a German-born theologian who interpreted the meaning of God and Jesus Christ in correlation with philosophical questions of modern life and thought. Wieman was an American Unitarian Universalist theologian who studied the process of human beings' ability to learn, grow, change, and perform to their highest potential.

## MARRIAGE AND CHILDREN

At Morehouse, at Crozer, and at Boston University, King took his studies seriously but also pursued an active social life. While attending college in Atlanta, he dated a young woman from a prominent black family whom his father expected him to marry. But King was not ready for marriage at that point. At Crozer, King and a young white woman fell in love. King considered marrying her, but a black local minister whom King had befriended advised him against it because of all the problems they would face in American society as an interracial couple. He reluctantly broke off the relationship. In Boston, King and his roommate enjoyed the nightlife at a local jazz club and formed a philosophy club with about a dozen other male and female black students who met on weekends at their apartment. But he was not particularly impressed by any of the young women he met.

By January 1952, King was ready to find a wife. He called up a female friend from Atlanta who was studying at the New England Conservatory of Music in Boston and asked her, "Do you know any nice, attractive young ladies?"[24] She gave him the phone number of another conservatory student, Coretta Scott. King called Scott, who agreed to have lunch with him the following day at the conservatory cafeteria. Scott, a native of Heiberger, near Marion, Alabama, had earned her undergraduate degree from Antioch College in Ohio and received a scholarship to study music at the New England Conservatory. A mezzo-soprano, her goal at that time was to become a concert singer.

"She talked about things other than music," King recalled of the conversation on their first date. "I never will forget, the first discussion we had was about the question of racial and economic injustice and the question of peace. She had been actively engaged in movements dealing with these problems."[25] King was so impressed with Scott, he made up his mind after only an hour that she had everything he ever wanted in a wife—"character, intelligence, personality, and beauty"[26]—and he wanted to marry her. In his autobiography, King said, "I didn't want a wife I couldn't communicate with. I had to have a wife who would be as dedicated as I was. I wish I could say that I led her down this path, but I must say we went down it together because she was as actively involved and concerned when we met as she is now."[27]

Although she was attracted to him from the start, Scott took longer than an hour to make up her mind about marrying King. The couple enjoyed many more dates, including walks in the park, ice skating, a concert, and a drive to the seashore. King expressed his concerns about Scott's career should she agree to marry him. He would expect her to become a full-time "preacher's wife" and mother of the children they would have, so she would have to give up the idea of being a concert singer. Even though it was more common in the 1950's for women in the United States to become full-time homemakers after marriage than to continue in a career outside the home, this choice was not an easy one for Scott. But her love for King was greater than her musical ambition, so she accepted his proposal. They agreed, however, that she would complete her music degree before taking on full responsibility for the home.

Daddy King at first brushed off his son's choice of bride, still hoping that M. L. would marry his former Atlanta girlfriend, but M. L.'s mind and heart were set on Scott. As Daddy King got to know her better, he warmed up to Scott and gave the couple his blessing to wed. He officiated at the ceremony on the spacious lawn of the Scott family home in Marion on June 18, 1953.

The newlyweds returned to Boston and moved into a four-room apartment. Martin, as he was known to his wife, finished up his coursework and started on his Ph.D. dissertation at Boston University School of Theology while Coretta maintained an even more demanding schedule to finish her final year of study at the New England Conservatory of Music, from which she would earn her degree in June 1954.

In the fall of 1953, King began to get job offers. The initial choices included three colleges and two churches, one in New York and one in Massachusetts. As he was pondering these offers, he received an invitation to preach at the Dexter Avenue Baptist Church in Montgomery, Alabama, which was looking for a new pastor. King delivered a guest sermon there on Jan. 24, 1954. He was well received, and the church's pulpit committee offered him the pastorate about a month later. In the meantime, King delivered a guest sermon at a church in Detroit that had expressed an interest in him. During the spring of 1954, Martin and Coretta pondered their options. They were tempted to remain in the North, where racial discrimination was less intense and there would be opportunities for Coretta to sing occasionally. But together they decided that Martin should take the Montgomery position, which he accepted on April 14. As King recalled in his autobiography, "The South, after all, was our home. Despite its shortcomings, we had a real desire to do something about the problems that we had felt so keenly as youngsters. Moreover, . . . we had the feeling that something remarkable was unfolding in the South, and we wanted to be on hand to witness it."[28]

They did not have to wait long for something remarkable. On May 17, 1954—just 15 days after King preached his first sermon

*King and his wife Coretta had four children. The two oldest, Yolanda, 5, and Martin Luther III, are shown playing the piano with their parents in the living room of their Atlanta home in 1960.*

as minister of the Dexter Avenue Baptist Church—the Supreme Court of the United States ruled unanimously in the case of *Brown v. Board of Education of Topeka* that segregation in public schools is unconstitutional. This ruling was an important first step in breaking down the "separate but equal" principle that was used to justify segregation in the South. On Sept. 1, 1954, Martin and Coretta moved into the church parsonage, a seven-room, white frame house with a railed-in front porch. Martin's official installation ceremony was held on October 31.

Reverend King quickly joined the local branch of the NAACP and insisted that every adult member of his church also join the NAACP and register to vote. He organized a social and political action committee within the church to keep the congregation informed about issues of importance to Montgomery's black community. King also joined the Alabama Council on Human Relations, the city's only truly interracial group, and was elected vice president of the council within a few months.

By early 1955, Martin and Coretta had settled into their new life in Montgomery, and Coretta became pregnant with the couple's first child, a girl born on November 17. They named her Yolanda Denise but called her Yoki. The couple would later have three more children: Martin Luther III, born Oct. 23, 1957; Dexter Scott, born Jan. 30, 1961; and Bernice Albertine, nicknamed Bunny, born March 28, 1963.

# Chapter 2: Early Civil Rights Activities

## MONTGOMERY BUS SYSTEM

By 1955, black riders on Montgomery's buses were getting fed up with the Jim Crow laws that required white and black passengers to sit in separate rows. Black passengers accounted for about 70 percent of the bus system's ridership, and sometimes they ended up standing in the aisle at the back of the bus while several rows of seats in front, reserved for white passengers only, remained empty. When all the seats in the front rows were full and additional white passengers boarded the bus, the black passengers were required to leave their seats in the next rows to make room for them. To make matters worse, all the bus drivers were white, and many of them treated the black riders disrespectfully, calling them such insulting names as "niggers," "black apes," and "black cows." In the spring and summer of 1955, several black passengers—one of them a 15-year-old girl, Claudette Colvin—on separate occasions defied the racial segregation law and were arrested, typically charged with "disorderly conduct," tried, convicted, and fined. Their cases attracted little public attention.

All that began to change in the late afternoon of Dec. 1, 1955, when a 42-year-old black seamstress named Rosa Parks refused to give up her seat to a white passenger on a bus she was riding home after work. Seated in the middle of the filled, 36-seat bus, Parks quietly declined to budge when the driver ordered her to stand up and make room for a white man to sit in her row. Speaking softly, she answered that she was not in the white section and therefore should not have to move. The driver stopped the bus and fetched the police, who arrested Parks. She was charged with violating the local segregation laws. E. D. Nixon, a leader in the Montgomery chapter of the NAACP, for which Parks served as secretary, signed the bond papers to release her from the jail at the police station. Her trial was set for December 5.

Once they arrived at the Parks home, Nixon told Parks that her case could be used to challenge the bus system's segregation law if she were willing to fight it. She agreed, and the lawyer whom Nixon called, Fred Gray, agreed to represent her. Gray then called his friend Jo Ann Robinson, an Alabama State University professor of English and president of the Women's Political Council, to tell her what was going on. Shortly after midnight on December 2, Robinson and other members of the council met secretly at the university to draft and run off thousands of mimeographed copies of a letter calling for a one-day boycott of the bus system on December 5 in support of Parks. Robinson called Nixon at about 3:00 a.m. to inform him of the council's plans to circulate the letter, and Nixon agreed to boycott. At about 5:00 a.m., Nixon called King to explain what had happened to Parks and suggest the boycott. The rest of the day was filled with phone calls. That evening, King presided over a meeting at his church of about 40 religious and civic leaders from Montgomery's black community, including his friend Ralph Abernathy, pastor of the First Baptist Church. The group agreed that it was time for action. L. Roy Bennett, president of the city's Interdenominational Ministerial Alliance, formally proposed the boycott. He appointed a committee that included King to prepare the group's statement, which said:

> *Don't ride the bus to work, to town, to school, or any place Monday, December 5. Another Negro woman has been arrested and put in jail because she refused to give up her bus seat. Don't ride the buses to work, to town, to school, or anywhere on Monday. If you work, take a cab, or share a ride, or walk. Come to a mass meeting, Monday at 7:00 p.m., at the Holt Street Baptist Church for further instruction.*[1]

On the morning of December 3, King and his church secretary ran off 7,000 mimeographed copies of the statement, and a volunteer army of women and young people distributed the leaflets all over town. King and other leaders contacted the city's 18 black taxicab companies and persuaded them to carry passengers for 10 cents (75 cents today), apiece—the price of bus fare—during the upcoming boycott. Altogether, the taxi companies had over 200 cabs. On December 4, an article about the planned boycott appeared in the Montgomery *Advertiser* newspaper. Nixon had tipped off the paper's city editor in the hope that a story about the boycott would help spread the word. It did, but the writer of the newspaper article also called the boycott a negative approach to the problem and even accused the NAACP of planting Parks on the bus to stir up trouble. After reflecting about the matter, King concluded that the boycott was simply an act of civil disobedience in the manner Thoreau had described: a large-scale withdrawal of cooperation from an evil system. Still, as he went to bed that night, he wondered whether it would work.

Martin and Coretta King were up and dressed by 5:30 a.m. on December 5. The South Jackson bus line ran down their street, normally carrying more black passengers than any other line in town, and the bus stop was only 5 feet (1.5 meters) from their house. The Kings had a clear view as the first bus rolled up to the stop. To their amazement and joy, it was completely empty. Fifteen minutes later, a second empty bus passed by. When a third bus arrived, it carried two white passengers and no black ones. King jumped in his car and spent nearly an hour driving around Montgomery, peering into each passing bus. He counted "no more than eight Negro passengers"[2] throughout the entire city. Considering that on a normal day there would be thousands, the cooperation rate was nearly 100 percent. Ironically, the Montgomery police contributed to the success of the boycott. The city's new police commissioner, a white man named Clyde Sellers, assumed that black riders would not stay off the buses unless they were threatened with violence by "Negro goon squads,"[3] so he ordered roving police squads to go out early that morning and intimidate the goons before they could intimidate the riders. However, there were no goons. The boycott was carried out without violence. And because they saw white police officers hovering around their bus stops, most of the few black passengers who had been planning to take the bus despite the boycott changed their minds and stayed away.

King interrupted his drive to attend the midmorning trial of Rosa Parks at the police court. As expected, the judge convicted her of disobeying the city segregation ordinance. She was fined $10 (about $75 today), plus $4 (about $29 today), in court costs. Gray immediately filed an appeal on behalf of his client, and Nixon once again posted bond for her release. A crowd of about 500 black supporters awaited her.

Bennett, King, Abernathy, Nixon, and a number of other black leaders met at 3:00 p.m. to prepare for the larger 7:00 p.m. meeting. Overjoyed at the initial success of the boycott, they decided to call for it to continue and to draw up a list of demands that the bus system would have to meet to end it. They formed the Montgomery Improvement Association (MIA) to oversee the boycott. King was nominated for president of the new organization and unanimously elected. Later that afternoon, as workers and students returned to their homes, the buses remained empty. Among the more creative alternative modes of transportation King noted were mules and horse-drawn buggies. For many of the people who walked, the distance was as far as 12 miles (19 kilometers) between downtown Montgomery and the black neighborhoods. As he watched them patiently trudging home, King recalled, he felt that "there is nothing more majestic than the determined courage of individuals willing to suffer and sacrifice for their freedom and dignity."[4]

About 15,000 people attended the evening meeting at the Holt Street Baptist Church in Montgomery. King had only 20 minutes to prepare his first speech as leader of the boycott. He quickly jotted down an outline of what he wanted to convey: a strong call to action with an equally strong affirmation of Christian love in practice. While television cameras whirred, King's baritone voice rang out as he told the crowd that "first and foremost, we are American citizens. . . . We are not here advocating violence. . . . The only weapon that we have . . . is the weapon of protest. . . . The great glory of American democracy is the right to protest for right."[5] His 16-minute speech was greeted with a standing ovation. Then Abernathy read the MIA resolution. It called for the boycott to continue until the bus lines and city officials agreed to three conditions: (1) to guarantee that bus drivers would treat black passengers courteously; (2) to seat passengers on a first-come, first-served basis, with black seating from the back of the bus toward the front and white seating from the front toward the back; and (3) to employ black drivers on predominantly black routes. Everyone present stood in favor of the motion. As King drove home later, he savored the feeling that no matter how long it took to achieve the three goals of the resolution, the unity of purpose and sense of dignity shown at the mass meeting that night meant that the victory was already won.

The boycott would last for 382 days. Although white representatives of the city and the bus company did meet with King and other MIA leaders in December 1955, they made no concessions. Furthermore, the police commissioner threatened to arrest cab drivers who failed to charge the legal minimum fare of 45 cents ($3.30 today), per passenger. The cab companies relented and ended their 10-cent fare agreement for the boycotters. In response, the MIA quickly organized a fleet of about 300 volunteer drivers, including the university professor Robinson, and distributed a list of 48 dispatch points and 42 pickup stations. In mid-December, a young white librarian named Juliette Morgan wrote a letter published in the *Advertiser* in which she sympathized with the boycotters and compared their struggle to that of Gandhi. This comparison underscored King's earlier belief in the value of combining Gandhi's method of nonviolence with the spirit of Christian love.

King's personal commitment to nonviolence was severely tested early in 1956. By late January, King was receiving dozens of hate letters and obscene phone calls every day. On January 26, he was arrested for driving 30 miles (48 kilometers) per hour in a 25-mile- (40-kilometer-) per-hour zone and detained for several hours in a crowded, filthy cell at the Montgomery City Jail. The arrest was part of the city's "get tough" campaign of harassing drivers in order to disrupt the volunteer car pool. But worse was yet to come. While King attended an MIA mass meeting the evening of January 30, a bomb exploded on the front porch at his house. When word of the bombing reached King, he rushed home. To his great relief, his wife and baby daughter were unharmed. Coretta's amazing composure calmed her husband, and he addressed the angry crowd that had gathered, urging them to "love our enemies" and remain nonviolent. In a letter quoted in the *New York Times* on February 24, King wrote, "This is not war between the white and the

Negro but a conflict between justice and injustice. . . . We are seeking to improve not the Negro of Montgomery but the whole of Montgomery. . . . We must have compassion and understanding for those who hate us. We must realize so many people are taught to hate us that they are not totally responsible for their hate." He concluded that "we are always on the threshold of a new dawn."[6]

On Feb. 21, 1956, the Montgomery County Grand Jury declared that those who were boycotting the buses were in violation of an old state law against boycotts. They indicted King and more than 100 other people. King was in Nashville giving a series of lectures at the time the indictments were announced. After he returned, he turned himself in at the county jail. He was tried and, on March 22, found guilty of violating the state antiboycott law. He was sentenced to either pay a $500 fine (about $3,600 today), or spend 386 days at hard labor. King's lawyers appealed the case.

King's Montgomery campaign won a small victory in the summer of 1956. In response to a lawsuit Gray had filed on February 2, a U.S. district court ruled on June 4 that racial segregation on city bus lines is unconstitutional. But attorneys for the city of Montgomery and the state of Alabama appealed the verdict to the U.S. Supreme Court, and the segregation continued in the meantime. On October 30, the city attorneys petitioned a state court to issue an order called an *injunction* against the car pool for operating a private transportation business without a license. A hearing was scheduled for November 13. That day, the judge granted the injunction to stop the car pool. But King's disappointment with that decision was far outweighed by his elation over another one handed down the same day: The U.S. Supreme Court affirmed the district court's decision declaring racial segregation on city buses unconstitutional. Soon the buses would be integrated, and the car pool would no longer be necessary. That night, 40 cars full of hooded Ku Klux Klan members drove through Montgomery's black neighborhoods in an effort to frighten the residents back into submission, but the people in those neighborhoods treated the procession like a circus parade and stood watching without showing fear, their homes' doors open and porch lights on. The next night, thousands of jubilant boycotters thronged

the Holt Street Baptist Church to celebrate. King joined in the celebration yet also warned the crowd not to be boastful or pushy when they got back on the buses but to simply sit wherever they found a vacant seat.

On Dec. 20, 1956, the Supreme Court mandate finally reached Montgomery, ordering the city to provide equal, integrated seating on public buses. The MIA scheduled a mass meeting that night to vote for an end to the boycott and prepare for a return to the buses the following day. On the morning of December 21, followed by newspaper reporters and television crews, King boarded the first bus that stopped outside his house. Joining him for the ride were Abernathy, Nixon, and Glenn Smiley, who was a white minister and member of the Fellowship of Reconciliation. The bus driver smiled and greeted all the passengers courteously. King took a seat in the front, next to Smiley. Downtown they transferred to another bus line that ran through white neighborhoods. They encountered a few hostile reactions to the integrated system among the white passengers, but most of the white riders responded calmly, and a few were even friendly. The success of the Montgomery bus boycott encouraged black leaders in the cities of Birmingham and Mobile, Alabama, as well as the city of Tallahassee, Florida, to launch similar protests. It also propelled King to national fame and identified him as a symbol of Southern blacks' new efforts to fight racial injustice.

## SOUTHERN CHRISTIAN LEADERSHIP CONFERENCE

Desegregation of Montgomery's bus system did not bring an end to racial tensions in the city. By late December 1956, there was a resurgence of violence against black citizens by white extremists. A shotgun blast ripped through the front door of King's house on December 22, but the family was unharmed. On Christmas Eve, a 15-year-old black girl was brutally beaten by five white men at a bus stop. Later in the month, whites armed with guns shot at buses. The Ku Klux Klan marched in the street and left burning crosses on the lawns of black families' homes. The violence escalated in the new year. In the wee hours of the morning on Jan. 10, 1957, bombs exploded at Abernathy's home and at First Baptist Church, along with four other churches in black neighborhoods. More bombs went off the morning of January 27, and an unexploded bomb made from 12 sticks of dynamite was found still smoldering on the front porch of King's house, where no one was home at the time. The bombings drew condemnation from white religious and civic leaders as well as black ones. On January 31, seven Klansmen were arrested in connection with the bombings. After these arrests, the bombings ceased. At their trial later in the spring, in which King was one of the witnesses called to testify, an all-white jury acquitted the first two men, disregarding their signed confessions. Charges were dropped against the remaining five.

On the morning that Abernathy's home and church were bombed, he was in Atlanta with King. The two men were there for a meeting with a group of about 60 black leaders from 10 Southern states who had gathered to establish a regional organization to help coordinate nonviolent protests and other civil rights work in the South. Abernathy—whose wife and daughter had escaped harm— and King flew back to Montgomery that morning to assess the damage, but King rejoined the meeting in Atlanta later. At the end of the meeting, on January 11, the group voted to form the Southern

Leaders Conference (later called the Southern Christian Leadership Conference, or SCLC). King was elected president of the conference at a meeting on February 14.

King's face appeared on the cover of *Time* magazine's Feb. 18, 1957, issue. The accompanying story commented on his rapid rise "from nowhere to become one of the nation's remarkable leaders of men."[7] This free publicity made him even more recognizable as he traveled around the country speaking on behalf of the SCLC. The following month, he went to Africa as one of the foreign dignitaries invited to celebrate the independence of Ghana from British rule on March 5. The next day, King and Michael Scott, an Anglican church leader, had a conversation in which they discussed the South African white-minority government's policy of rigid racial separation, called *apartheid*, and compared it to segregation in the American South. On his way home, King stopped in British-controlled Nigeria and was appalled at the squalid living conditions of the black Africans in that country. This trip abroad fostered in King a heightened awareness of the numerous independence movements going on in Africa, which he followed with interest for the rest of his life.

On May 17, 1957—the third anniversary of the Supreme Court's *Brown* decision that declared segregation in public schools unconstitutional—a large group of black activists and some white supporters from around the nation held the Prayer Pilgrimage in front of the Lincoln Memorial in Washington, D.C. Standing before the huge statue of the president who nearly 100 years earlier had issued the Emancipation Proclamation that led to the end of slavery in the United States, King addressed a crowd estimated between 15,000 and 37,000 people. He started off by praising the Brown decision as "a reaffirmation of the good old American doctrine of freedom and equality for all people." However, he went on to say that "all types of conniving methods are still being used to prevent Negroes from becoming registered voters. The denial of this sacred right is a tragic betrayal of the highest mandates of our democratic traditions and it

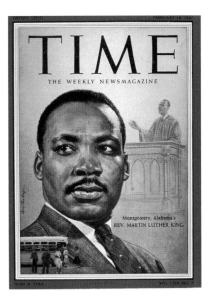

King's face appeared on the cover of Time magazine on Feb. 18, 1957, shown above. The cover story commented on King's rise "to become one of the nation's remarkable leaders of men." King appeared on the magazine's cover again, on Jan. 3, 1964, as Time's 1963 Man of the Year.

*On May 17, 1957, the third anniversary of the Supreme Court's* Brown v. Board of Education of Topeka *decision declaring racial segregation in public schools unconstitutional, King addressed a crowd of thousands at the Prayer Pilgrimage at the Lincoln Memorial in Washington, D.C.*

is democracy turned upside down. . . . So our most urgent request to the president of the United States and every member of Congress is to give us the right to vote. . . . Give us the ballot and we will transform the salient misdeeds of bloodthirsty mobs into the calculated good deeds of orderly citizens."[8] King and other civil rights leaders got their chance to meet with President Dwight D. Eisenhower more than a year later, on June 23, 1958, but derived little satisfaction from the president's unwillingness to consider any of the group's suggestions for improving civil rights. In the meantime, the U.S. Congress had passed the first civil rights bill in 82 years on Sept. 9, 1957, after a lengthy debate in the Senate. The Civil Rights Act of 1957 created the Civil Rights Commission to investigate charges of the denial of civil rights and established the Civil Rights Division in the Department of Justice to enforce federal civil rights laws and regulations.

In 1958, King got another taste of jail and had another brush with death. On September 3, Martin and Coretta King made their way through a crowd toward a courtroom at Montgomery Courthouse with Abernathy, who was going to attend the preliminary hearing in the case of a man who had tried to kill him with a hatchet at Abernathy's office at First Baptist Church in Montgomery a few days earlier. The white guard at the door would let only Abernathy in. King persisted, asking for his lawyer, Fred Gray, who was inside the courtroom. The guard, to whom the black man in the tan suit and fedora hat was just another "boy," became angry and summoned two white policemen. They grabbed King roughly from behind, pinning his right arm behind his back, and hauled him out the door and around the corner to the police station. King warned Coretta to stay back as she hurried after them, but a photographer who happened by at that moment did follow them into the station, snapping away on his camera. The policemen hustled King up to the booking desk, his arm still pinned behind him. Then they took him down a dim hallway, out of the photographer's sight, where they choked him, searched him, and booted him into an empty cell. As King waited, wondering what would happen next, a lieutenant he knew walked by and promised he would not let anyone bother him further. Soon the two policemen returned, subdued, and led King back to the front desk, where he was charged with insulting an officer and released on his own bond. By the next day, the international wire services had distributed the photographer's pictures of King's rough handling by the police, and the public reaction was one of outrage.

On September 5, with the national press on hand, King was tried by a judge in Montgomery, found guilty of loitering and refusing to obey a police officer, and ordered to pay $14 (about $94 today), or serve 14 days in jail. To the judge's surprise, King chose jail. He asked to read a statement, which the judge allowed. Echoing the words of Gandhi, who had been in a similar situation years before him, King declared, "Your Honor, I could not in all good conscience pay a fine for an act that I did not commit and above all for brutal treatment that I did not deserve. . . . The time has come when perhaps only the willing and nonviolent acts of suffering by the innocent can arouse this nation to wipe out the scourge of brutality and violence inflicted upon Negroes who seek only to walk with dignity before God and Man."[9] As he waited in the holding area to be transferred to the jail, the judge informed him that an anonymous person had paid his fine. King was released. His anonymous benefactor turned out to be the unrepentant segregationist Montgomery police commissioner, Clyde Sellers, who claimed he merely wanted to save the taxpayers the expense of feeding King in jail for 14 days. In condemning King's courtroom statement as a "publicity stunt," however, it was clear that what he really wanted was to avoid 14 more days of bad publicity for the Montgomery police department.

Soon afterward, on Sept. 20, 1958, King made an appearance at Blumstein's department store in Harlem, a large black neighborhood in New York City, to sign copies of his recently published first book, *Stride Toward Freedom: The Montgomery Story.* A 42-year-old black woman named Izola Ware Curry approached the desk where he sat and asked, "Are you Martin Luther King?" King replied, "Yes." Suddenly he felt something sharp plunge into his chest. The woman had just pulled out a razor-sharp, 7-inch- (17.5-centimeter-) long letter opener and stabbed him. As King sat stunned, the weapon still protruding from his chest, Curry started shrieking obscenities about King as security guards grabbed her. King was taken to Harlem Hospital, where an interracial team of surgeons carefully extracted the blade that had lodged between his heart and lung. Its tip had touched the aorta, the large artery leading from the heart. The chief surgeon later told King that if he had so much as sneezed before the surgery, the aorta would have been punctured and he would have drowned in his own blood. This information was later published in the *New York Times,* and a white ninth-grade girl from New York responded with a memorable letter to King in which she concluded, "I'm so happy that you didn't sneeze."[10]

King's would-be assassin, who had also been carrying a loaded gun tucked inside her blouse, was diagnosed as a paranoid schizophrenic. Curry apparently had become aware of King through his media coverage and decided to blame this famous man for all of her own problems. King declined to press charges against Curry and requested that she receive treatment for her mental illness. She was committed to the state hospital for the criminally insane. King was released from Harlem Hospital on October 3. He kept a low profile for the rest of the year as he recovered at home, canceling all travel plans and public appearances. His only speeches were sermons from the pulpit at his church. King used this unusually quiet period in his life to read, reflect, and reenergize himself for the struggles he knew lay ahead.

On Feb. 3, 1959, Martin and Coretta King left for a trip to India, accompanied by Martin's friend and biographer Lawrence Reddick. They spent about a month touring the country as the invited guests of Indian Prime Minister Jawaharlal Nehru. The Montgomery bus boycott had been well publicized in India, and Martin found the people there keenly interested in his views on racial problems. They also enjoyed hearing Coretta sing. King noted the stark contrast between the lives of the poor people crowded into slums and the wealthy who lived luxuriously on large estates. But he was impressed by the way India's leaders were attempting to grapple with the nation's social and economic problems. The Kings went to the place where Gandhi began his famous salt march to the sea in 1930, and they talked with many of the great Indian leader's relatives and friends. King reflected in his autobiography:

> I left India more convinced than ever before that nonviolent resistance was the most potent weapon available to oppressed people in their struggle for freedom. . . . The way of acquiescence leads to moral and spiritual suicide. The way of violence leads to bitterness in the survivors and brutality in the destroyers. But the way of nonviolence leads to redemption and the creation of the beloved community.[11]

King returned to the American civil rights movement with renewed vigor. In the fall of 1959, the SCLC decided for 1960 to concentrate on increasing the number of black registered voters throughout the South. King also wanted the SCLC to set up a program to teach people effective techniques of nonviolent protest against various forms of segregation in their communities. Realizing that these plans to increase SCLC activity would require more of his time and involvement, King decided that he should live closer to the organization's headquarters in Atlanta. On Feb. 1, 1960, King and his family moved to Atlanta, where he rejoined his father as co-pastor of Ebenezer Baptist Church.

## SIT-INS AND OTHER PEACEFUL PROTESTS

As King began to resettle his family in Atlanta on Feb. 2, 1960, four black male freshmen from North Carolina A&T College (now North Carolina Agricultural and Technical State University) walked into a Woolworth's five-and-ten-cent store in downtown Greensboro and sat at the lunch counter. They ordered coffee but were refused service because only whites were allowed to sit at the counter. But the young men sat patiently, waiting to be served, until the store closed for the evening. Word of this peaceful protest spread rapidly around town. The next day, the four black students returned to sit at the lunch counter, accompanied by 19 others. The following day, the group numbered 85. By the end of the week, hundreds of black students and even some white students were participating in the protest, taking turns sitting at the lunch counter so that they would not all miss their classes. Soon black college students across the South began sitting at lunch counters and entering other places of business that refused to serve blacks. By the end of February, sit-in campaigns were taking place in 31 cities across eight Southern states.

King was excited by the news of what the students were doing. He admired their willingness to actively challenge the segregation laws in a nonviolent way. But his attention was diverted from the sit-ins on February 17, when he was arrested on charges of falsifying his Alabama state income tax returns for 1956 and 1958. King was dismayed. He realized that the only way to clear his name from this attack on his character was to win the case in court, but he doubted that an all-white jury in Montgomery would declare him innocent. Still, he resolved to try. The trial would not take place until May, and in the meantime, he could return to his work in supporting the student protesters.

The students needed all the help they could get. In Nashville in late February, hostile white crowds surrounded the student protesters and heckled them, beat them, threw rocks at them, and poked them with lighted cigarettes, all while indifferent white policemen looked on and did not stop the abuse. The students did not fight back. Nevertheless, the police then arrested the students for violating

the segregation law and took them to jail. At their trials, where they were pronounced guilty, more than a dozen of the students followed the lead of King and Gandhi in choosing to go to jail rather than pay a fine. Sixty others, moved by their fellow students' courage, summoned their own and joined them. Another wave of protesters began a new round of sit-ins, prompting the mayor of Nashville to offer them a deal: If they stopped the sit-ins, he would release the jailed students and establish a biracial committee to address the issue of segregation at downtown stores. They accepted. Their protest stopped, but other nonviolent student protests began in 40 more Southern cities in March.

The most dramatic stories about racial confrontations in the spring of 1960 came not from the South but from South Africa, where masses of black Africans were carrying out peaceful protests against the country's apartheid laws. On March 21, police at Sharpeville (now part of Vereeniging), near Johannesburg, fired their guns at an unarmed crowd of protesters and killed 67 black Africans. The Sharpeville massacre, as it became known, drew international condemnation and set off rioting throughout South Africa. The South African government outlawed the main opposition groups, forcing the nonviolent resistance leader Nelson Mandela into hiding. Unlike King and Gandhi, Mandela would reluctantly abandon his nonviolent strategy for a time in response to his government's increasing brutality.

Back in the United States, King spoke on April 15, 1960, at a weekend conference at Shaw University in Raleigh, North Carolina. About 200 students from about 40 communities throughout 10 states had gathered there to organize student civil rights activities. King offered to help them establish a youth branch of the SCLC, but they chose to create their own organization, which they called the Student Nonviolent Coordinating Committee (SNCC). James Lawson, a theology student who played a leading role in organizing the SNCC, taught the students how to peacefully tolerate the insults they were likely to receive and how to position their bodies to better withstand beatings from angry white crowds or police. Soon more than 70,000 students were participating in sit-ins all over the South.

For his tax evasion trial in May, King mustered the finest legal defense team he could find, led by William Ming of Chicago and Hubert Delaney of New York City. For three days, King's lawyers doggedly presented evidence and examined witnesses in an effort to convince the all-white jury of their black client's innocence. On May 28, after several hours of deliberation, the jury rendered its verdict: not guilty. Relieved and amazed, King recalled that "on this occasion I learned that truth and conviction in the hands of a skillful advocate could make what started out as a bigoted, prejudiced jury, choose the path of justice."[12]

By August 1960, the sit-ins reportedly had succeeded in ending segregation at lunch counters in 27 Southern cities. King himself joined the sit-in campaign on October 19 in Atlanta. He walked into Rich's department store downtown with a group of about 75 students and sat at the whites-only lunch counter. They were all arrested on the charge of trespassing and taken to the Fulton County Jail. Tried and convicted, they all chose jail over a fine. Several days later, the prisoners were informed that the charges had been dropped and that the downtown merchants were willing to desegregate their lunch counters. All the students were released, but King was not. Instead, he was transferred to DeKalb County, Georgia, where he was charged with violating his probation from a previous arrest for driving without a Georgia license. That arrest had occurred a few months after he moved to Atlanta from Alabama, and he had forgotten to get a license for his new state of residence. King insisted he had paid a fine, but he did not realize his lawyer had actually pleaded guilty on his behalf and King's sentence also included a probation period that required him to avoid further arrests. On October 25, the Georgia judge found him guilty and sentenced him to four months hard labor. King was shocked. In the middle of the night, guards took him from his cell, shackled his wrists and ankles, and drove him to Reidsville State Prison—hundreds of miles (or kilometers) away in the middle of a Ku Klux Klan stronghold. There they locked him in a cold cell infested with cockroaches. The food was inedible. But on October 28, he was suddenly released. Coretta explained that she had received a solicitous call from Senator John F. Kennedy, the Democratic presidential nominee, who had heard about King's incarceration.

King had met with Kennedy back in June and had a productive conversation with him, although King told Kennedy at the time that he never publicly endorsed political candidates. Senator Kennedy and his brother, Robert F. Kennedy, investigated the situation and convinced the judge to reverse his decision and release King on bond. King made a public statement thanking—though still not endorsing—Senator Kennedy. Thousands of black voters nevertheless cast their ballots for Kennedy, who on November 8 defeated his Republican opponent, Vice President Richard M. Nixon, by fewer than 115,000 popular votes. Robert F. Kennedy became attorney general.

Civil rights protests expanded further in the early 1960's. In mid-May 1961, a group of nonviolent black and white Freedom Riders from the Congress of Racial Equality (CORE) entered Montgomery, Alabama, by bus to test local segregation laws. As a result of two prior U.S. Supreme Court decisions, segregation on interstate buses and in bus terminals had been banned, but many Southern bus stations defiantly remained segregated. When the Freedom Riders got off the bus in Montgomery, white rioters attacked them. King went to Montgomery on May 21 to address a mass meeting at Ralph

Abernathy's church in support of the Freedom Riders. White rioters outside hurled rocks and tear gas through the church windows. From a telephone in the basement, King called Attorney General Kennedy, who sent U.S. marshals to the city to help restore order. Freedom Rides continued throughout the South all summer. Finally, at Kennedy's urging, the Interstate Commerce Commission (ICC) in September issued regulations ending segregation at bus facilities as of November 1. Southern stations slowly began to comply.

King's civil rights work often took him away from Atlanta and his family for extended periods. He tried to make up for quantity of time with quality, playing and talking with the children as much as possible when he was home. By the time Yoki was 6, King found himself in the same painful position his parents once had been, having to explain racism to his daughter so she would understand why she could not go to Funtown, a local amusement park that was advertised on television but closed to black children.

Major demonstrations occurred in Albany, Georgia, in 1961 and 1962. King was among the black leaders working with the protesters, and he was arrested twice during the Albany campaign. Altogether he spent several weeks in jail. But the Albany campaign on the whole was unsuccessful. City government officials refused to make any concessions. The boycotted bus line simply shut down. The savvy police chief refrained from using violence in arrests of protesters, so the public was less sympathetic to their efforts. Factional squabbles among some of the black leaders hampered cooperation within the group and fractured the support of the black community. Worst of all, violence erupted one night after police officers brutally beat a pregnant woman who was trying to bring food to jailed protesters. In retaliation, an angry black mob of about 2,000 people threw rocks and bottles at the police. Throughout the Albany campaign, federal officials for the most part kept their distance. King became increasingly unhappy that President Kennedy was doing little to advance civil rights.

# Chapter 3: Major Victories for King and the Civil Rights Movement, 1963–1965

## 1963: BIRMINGHAM AND WASHINGTON, D.C.

Early in 1963, Martin Luther King, Jr., and his SCLC associates launched massive demonstrations to protest racial discrimination in Birmingham, Alabama, a place King considered "the most segregated city in America."[1] King's assistance had been sought by Fred Shuttlesworth, the founder of the Alabama Christian Movement for Human Rights, an organization affiliated with the SCLC. Learning from the mistakes of the Albany campaign, King and those who worked with him, including Ralph Abernathy, spent nearly a year thinking about and then carefully planning what they would do in Birmingham. The SCLC conducted workshops on non-violence, recruited volunteers, and secured funding for bail bonds so that protesters who were arrested could be bailed out of jail in order to return to the protests.

On April 3, King issued a declaration of intention, called a *manifesto,* warning that demonstrations and boycotts would occur until certain demands were met, including that downtown stores desegregate their lunch counters, rest rooms, and drinking fountains; that local businesses hire black workers; and that city officials establish a biracial committee to work out a schedule for desegregation in other aspects of city life. Theophilus Eugene "Bull" Connor, who had recently claimed the office of mayor after disputing the mayoral election in which he lost, was a staunch segregationist and thus refused to consider any of the demands. And so the protests began. Some demonstrators conducted sit-ins at lunch counters downtown and at the library. Others marched in the streets, singing freedom songs. By April 10, about 300 protesters had gone to jail. That day, Connor obtained an injunction from a state court judge against King, Abernathy, Shuttlesworth, and other organizers. The injunction ordered them to cease the protests until their right to demonstrate had been argued in court. King decided, for the first time in his life, to disobey a court order. On April 11, he issued a statement that began, "We cannot in all good conscience obey such an injunction which is an unjust, undemocratic, and unconstitutional misuse of the legal process."[2] He and Abernathy prepared to lead a demonstration the following day, the Christian holy day of Good Friday, knowing that they would be arrested. That night, he found out that the bail money had run out. Not knowing where his campaign would get more money, he resolved to carry out his plan even if it meant having to stay in jail indefinitely for lack of funds.

As expected, King and Abernathy were arrested on Good Friday, April 12, and hauled off to jail. King was placed in solitary confinement, cut off from all contact with the outside world, in a cramped, dark cell containing only a metal bedspring with no mattress or bedding and a filthy toilet with no seat. Such isolation was a new experience for him, and he found it more difficult to endure than if his jailers had beaten him. Nelson Mandela, who at that moment was incarcerated in a dreadful South African prison for inciting antiapartheid strikes, likely would have sympathized. Saturday came and went, and then Easter Sunday dawned, the light of the new day barely visible through the high, barred window of King's cell. Finally, in the afternoon, two of his lawyers were permitted to visit him, with word that another would come the next day. Outside the jail, King's brother, A. D. King, who was pastor of a church in Birmingham, was leading the largest protest march of the campaign—1,500 prayerful participants. On April 15, the imprisoned King's lawyer brought good news: King's friend Harry Belafonte, a popular singer who supported the civil rights movement, had raised $50,000, for bail bonds and was willing to raise more if needed. Then the guards brought King a mattress and pillow, let him out briefly to exercise and shower, and permitted him to call his wife. Suspicious of the sudden improvement in his treatment, King discovered that Coretta had called Attorney General Robert Kennedy, who promised to investigate the situation. Both Attorney General Kennedy and his brother, President John Kennedy, called officials in Birmingham. Aware that they were being watched from Washington, King's jailers eased up on the harshness of his conditions.

Also that day, Connor's earlier mayoral election opponent, Albert Boutwell, on appeal in court was declared the winner and sworn in as mayor. Boutwell was also a segregationist but a more moderate one than Connor. King opted to remain in jail a few days longer. In a newspaper that one of his lawyers had managed to smuggle in for him, King read a statement signed by eight white Christian and Jewish clergymen from Alabama that praised the police and criticized the protesters as "extremists."

Indignant that these supposed men of God would oppose him on religious grounds, King drafted an open letter in response, using a pen smuggled in by his lawyers and writing first on scraps of the newspaper and later on a notepad he was allowed to receive. What he ended up with after several days of scribbling amounted to 20 pages when it was later typed out. It was titled "Letter from a Birmingham Jail." To the clergymen's charge that King was an "outsider" coming in to stir up trouble, he responded, "I cannot sit idly by in Atlanta and not be concerned about what happens in Birmingham. Injustice anywhere is a threat to justice everywhere."[3] He then explained in great detail how and why a nonviolent campaign is conducted. He went on to express his twin disappointments that (1) white moderates had not shown more concern for social justice and (2) most white churches had failed to grasp the moral rightness of integration, which he thought should be easy to see from the Christian point of view that all people are God's children, as exemplified by Jesus Christ, "an extremist for love, truth, and goodness."[4] But King wrapped up the letter in a positive way:

> One day the South will know that when these disinherited children of God sat down at lunch counters they were in reality standing up for the best in the American dream and the most sacred values in our Judeo-Christian heritage, and thusly, carrying our whole nation back to those great wells of democracy which were dug deep by the Founding Fathers in the formulation of the Constitution and the Declaration of Independence. . . . Let us all hope that the dark clouds of racial prejudice will soon pass away and the deep fog of misunderstanding will be lifted from our fear-drenched communities and in some not too distant tomorrow the radiant stars of love and

*brotherhood will shine over our great nation with all of their scintillating beauty.*

> *Yours for the cause of Peace and Brotherhood,*
> *Martin Luther King, Jr.*[5]

King's "Letter from a Birmingham Jail" was first published by the American Friends Service Committee, a Quaker organization committed to nonviolence and social equality, in the form of a pamphlet. It was reprinted as an essay in a number of periodicals, including *Christian Century, Liberation,* and *New Leader,* and later in King's book *Why We Can't Wait* (1964).

The Birmingham campaign continued throughout the spring of 1963. On May 2, more than 1,000 children took to the streets to demonstrate, singing as they marched. They were arrested and jailed. Many of them had earlier attended mass meetings and training sessions in which they learned the same techniques of nonviolent resistance used by the adult protesters, and they were eager to join the civil rights movement that for some youngsters had been going on their whole lives. The next day, more than 2,500 children showed up to march in the demonstrations. The numbers continued to swell throughout the week. Some parents went with their children to jail. Large numbers of older people joined in. May 6 went on record as the largest single day of arrests of nonviolent protesters in U.S. history. Throughout these demonstrations, police unleashed snarling dogs and blasted forceful streams of water from fire hoses to drive back peaceful protesters, including the children. Heavy news coverage of the violence produced a national outcry against segregation. On May 8, Birmingham's white business leaders told King they were ready to negotiate a settlement. The protest leaders suspended the demonstrations during the negotiations. On May 10, an agreement was reached that met the basic demands King had laid out in the manifesto. The protest campaign was over.

King returned to Atlanta on May 11 to spend Mother's Day, May 12, with his mother. Late the night of May 11, following a Ku Klux Klan meeting on the outskirts of Birmingham, bombs exploded in the city at A. D. King's house and at the Gaston Hotel, where the SCLC leaders had been staying during the Birmingham campaign.

The bombs went off just as the bars in the black neighborhoods were closing, and the thousands of tavern patrons who filled the streets quickly turned into a rioting mob. Alabama's segregationist governor, George C. Wallace, had his state police waiting to confront the rioters. When word of the riots reached M. L. King, he swiftly returned to Birmingham to calm the crowds and assure the white businessmen that the agreement would be honored. On the evening of May 12, President Kennedy announced on national television that he would not let "extremists"—meaning the KKK and other segregationists—jeopardize the agreement reached in Birmingham. To show he meant what he said, the president ordered 3,000 federal troops into position near the city and prepared to federalize the Alabama National Guard. The violence stopped. On May 20, the U.S. Supreme Court ruled that Birmingham's segregation ordinances were unconstitutional. On June 11, President Kennedy proposed a wide-ranging civil rights bill to the U.S. Congress.

King and other civil rights leaders then organized a massive march in Washington, D.C. The purpose of the event, called the March on Washington, was to bring attention to unemployment among black workers and to urge Congress to pass President Kennedy's civil rights bill. On Aug. 28, 1963, more than 200,000 Americans, including many whites as well as blacks, gathered at the Lincoln Memorial in the capital. It was the largest demonstration of the American civil rights movement. The high point of the rally, King's stirring "I Have a Dream" speech, eloquently defined the moral basis of the movement. Following are excerpts from King's famous speech.

> *I say to you today, my friends, so even though we face the difficulties of today and tomorrow, I still have a dream. It is a dream deeply rooted in the American dream.*
>
> *I have a dream that one day this nation will rise up and live out the true meaning of its creed: "We hold these truths to be self-evident; that all men are created equal." I have a dream that one day on the red hills of Georgia the sons of former slaves and the sons of former slaveowners will be able to sit down together at the table of brotherhood.*

*I have a dream that my four little children will one day live in a nation where they will not be judged by the color of their skin but by the content of their character.*

*This is our hope. This is the faith that I go back to the South with. With this faith we will be able to hew out of the mountain of despair a stone of hope. With this faith we will be able to transform the jangling discords of our nation into a beautiful symphony of brotherhood.*

*With this faith we will be able to work together, to pray together, to struggle together, to go to jail together, to stand up for freedom together, knowing that we will be free one day.*

*And this will be the day. This will be the day when all of God's children will be able to sing with new meaning, "My country 'tis of thee, sweet land of liberty, of thee I sing. Land where my fathers died, land of the Pilgrims' pride, from every mountainside, let freedom ring."*

*And if America is to be a great nation, this must become true. So let freedom ring from the prodigious hilltops of New Hampshire. Let freedom ring from the mighty mountains of New York. Let freedom ring from the heightening Alleghenies of Pennsylvania!*

*Let freedom ring from the snowcapped Rockies of Colorado! Let freedom ring from the curvaceous slopes of California! But not only that; let freedom ring from Stone Mountain of Georgia! Let freedom ring from Lookout Mountain of Tennessee! Let freedom ring from every hill and every molehill of Mississippi. From every mountainside, let freedom ring.*

*And when this happens, and when we allow freedom to ring, when we let it ring from every village and every hamlet, from every state and every city, we will be able to speed up that day when all of God's children, black men and white men, Jews and Gentiles, Protestants and Catholics, will be able to join hands and sing in the words of the old Negro spiritual, "Free at last! Free at last! Thank God Almighty, we are free at last!"*[6]

Still energized by the success of the March on Washington, King returned to Atlanta and resumed his duties as pastor of Ebenezer Baptist Church. After preaching at the Sunday morning church service on September 15, King received word that a bomb made of dynamite had just exploded at the Sixteenth Street Baptist Church in

*King led the 1963 March on Washington from the Washington Monument to the Lincoln Memorial. The high point of the massive rally, King's stirring "I Have a Dream" speech, eloquently defined the moral basis of the civil rights movement.*

Birmingham. Four girls had been killed in the blast, which blew a hole in the side of the church and shattered the face of Jesus Christ out of a stained-glass window. The girls—11-year-old Denise McNair and 14-year-olds Addie Mae Collins, Carole Robertson, and Cynthia Wesley had been in the women's lounge, getting dressed in white as they prepared to usher at the church's youth day service. The bomb had been planted the night before in the bushes outside the building, near the room where the girls would be preparing, and detonated by remote control. Overcome by grief and bitterness at the news of the bombing, King rushed to Birmingham, where riots had erupted in reaction to the incident. Governor Wallace's state troopers kept the city barely under control. The bombing would remain officially unsolved until November 1977, when Robert "Dynamite Bob" Chambliss, a Klansman and former mineworker skilled in the use of explosives—arrested as a suspect in 1963 but released—was convicted of first-degree murder in a local trial. On Sept. 22, 1963, King delivered a eulogy at a joint service for three of the slain girls in which he called them "martyred heroines of a holy crusade for freedom and human dignity." He asserted, "God still has a way of wringing the good out of evil. History has proven over and over again that unmerited suffering is redemptive. The innocent blood of these little girls may well serve as the redemptive force that will bring new light to this dark city. . . . Indeed, this tragic event may cause the white South to come to terms with its conscience."[7] But that day, the white South's conscience stayed home. A handful of white ministers were the only white people to attend the funeral.

Whites and blacks alike were stunned exactly two months later, on Nov. 22, 1963, when President Kennedy was shot to death by an assassin as he rode in an open limousine through the streets of Dallas. Vice President Lyndon B. Johnson was sworn in as president soon after Kennedy died. On November 27, in his first address to the U.S. Congress as president, Johnson urged passage of Kennedy's civil rights bill. In mid-December, the city council of Atlanta at last rescinded "all ordinances which require the separation of persons because of race, color, or creed,"[8] and King finally took his daughter Yoki to Funtown amusement park.

## 1964: CIVIL RIGHTS ACT AND NOBEL PEACE PRIZE

Martin Luther King, Jr., once again appeared on the cover of *Time* magazine. In its first issue of the new year, dated Jan. 3, 1964, the magazine proclaimed King its Man of the Year for 1963. But King was not one to rest on his laurels. He saw far more work ahead in the struggle for civil rights.

King's next challenge lay in the coastal city of St. Augustine, Florida, the oldest permanent settlement established in the United States by Europeans. Founded by the Spanish in 1565, the city became an important tourist resort in the 1880's. By the 1960's, it had also become one of the most militantly segregationist cities in the nation. On Feb. 9, 1964, Robert Hayling, a black local civil rights leader, requested help from the SCLC in his struggle. To the SCLC leaders who arrived, St. Augustine seemed like a battle zone—with nearly all of the fighting being done by an active group of more than 1,000 Ku Klux Klansmen and their supporters. Klansmen regularly bombed and shot into homes and businesses of black citizens, including Hayling. Such attacks went largely ignored by the local police, who brutally beat and jailed black demonstrators. King and the

SCLC nevertheless decided to launch a nonviolent protest campaign in St. Augustine.

For several months, hundreds of peaceful protesters spent their days challenging segregation policies at the city's beaches, restaurants, and other public accommodations, and their nights marching in the old Slave Market in St. Augustine's public square. As they marched, white crowds hurled insults, bricks, and bottles at them. On the night of May 28, Klansmen descended upon the marchers in the market and assaulted them with iron pipes and bicycle chains. The police looked on indifferently at first but eventually halted the violence after one of the SCLC leaders, Andrew Young, was beaten unconscious and left lying in the street. That night, King tried to reach President Johnson to request federal protection for the protesters. But Johnson was not as responsive as Kennedy had been. White House officials told King that the administration believed state and local authorities could handle the problem. The local sheriff's solution to the problem was to secure a local court injunction against night marches. King and his lawyers petitioned the U.S. District Court in Jacksonville, Florida, to overrule the local court's decision. In the meantime, King attempted to open a dialogue with white civic leaders. On June 9, the Jacksonville court ordered the sheriff and the city of St. Augustine to stop interfering with the marches and also prohibited the sheriff and his men from beating or otherwise harming those they arrested. But the protests and the Klan's brutal attacks on the night marchers continued. By the end of June, Florida Governor Farris Bryant stepped in and established an emergency biracial committee to facilitate negotiations between white and black leaders in St. Augustine so that they could reach a settlement. The demonstrations stopped.

The civil rights movement won a major victory on July 2, 1964, when President Johnson signed the Civil Rights Act of 1964. The law was passed by the U.S. Congress after a 75-day *filibuster* (lengthy debate to block legislation) in the Senate. The Civil Rights Act bans discrimination because of a person's color, race, national origin, religion, or sex. The rights protected by the act include the freedom to seek employment; vote; and use hotels, parks, restaurants, and other public places. The act authorizes the Office of Education (now the

Department of Education) to direct school desegregation programs in areas specified by the government. Furthermore, the government can sue any school system that refuses to desegregate or whose desegregation program the government considers inadequate. King and many other black leaders, including Rosa Parks, witnessed the signing. Johnson gave King a pen he used to sign the historic law. Although the Civil Rights Act of 1964 became—and even today remains—one of the nation's strongest civil rights laws, King knew that its passage would not suddenly eliminate all racial discrimination in the United States. He believed that the new law's section on voting rights was not clear enough to prevent further abuses, and the law did not address the issue of fair housing at all. Still, it was a huge stride forward.

Racial tensions boiled over in the North as well as the South during the long, hot summer of 1964. Black rioting in Harlem and in Newark, New Jersey, erupted in mid-July. King went to Harlem to urge the rioters to practice nonviolent resistance. In an ironic twist echoing the Birmingham campaign, local *black* leaders called King an "outsider" and rejected his attempts to help them. They also displayed an anti-Semitic attitude that alarmed King, who vowed to "uphold the fair name of Jews" because "bigotry in any form is an affront to us all."[9] Northern riots would break out again in August in black areas of Chicago; Philadelphia, Pennsylvania; and Jersey City, New Jersey.

After his visit to Harlem, King returned to the South. On July 20, the SCLC joined the SNCC, CORE, the NAACP, the Council of Federated Organizations (COFO), and the Mississippi Freedom Democratic Party (MFDP) in a massive campaign to increase black voter registration throughout Mississippi. It was a daunting task in a state where black churches and homes were regularly set on fire, and black citizens were often attacked and sometimes even murdered. But King believed that the only way to alleviate the suffering of these black citizens was to secure their right to vote. Then they would have the power to choose public officials who would protect, rather than disregard, their basic human and legal rights. On August 4, the bullet-riddled bodies of three civil rights workers from the campaign—

one black man, James Chaney, and two white Jewish men, Andrew Goodman and Michael Schwerner—were unearthed near Philadelphia, Mississippi, by FBI agents who had been searching for them since their mysterious disappearance on June 21. Months later, the FBI arrested the sheriff and deputy sheriff of Philadelphia and nearly two dozen local white men, most of them KKK members, for the murder of the three civil rights workers.

*King holds a picture of slain civil rights workers, Michael Schwerner, James Chaney, and Andrew Goodman,* shown left to right, *during a press conference in 1964. The men were involved in a campaign to increase black voter registration in Mississippi. The bullet-riddled bodies of the three men were found near Philadelphia, Mississippi.*

King became more politically involved than usual as the 1964 presidential election approached. He was disappointed that the Republican Party chose to nominate Senator Barry Goldwater of Arizona as its candidate for president. King believed that Goldwater was far too conservative to deal effectively with the pressing social and economic issues facing the country, and he feared that Goldwater's philosophy would aid racists. Departing from his typical nonpartisan stance, King urged blacks and whites alike to vote against Goldwater. On August 22, King spoke at the Democratic Party's national convention in Atlantic City, New Jersey. President Johnson, the party's nominee, won reelection in November in a landslide.

On Dec. 10, 1964, King experienced one of the proudest moments of his life as he accepted the Nobel Peace Prize in Oslo, Norway. At 35, he was the youngest person ever to receive the award. King was the third black person to win the Nobel Peace Prize. The first was the American statesman Ralph Bunche, who won the 1950 prize for his leading role in negotiations during the Arab-Israeli dispute of the late 1940's. The second was Albert John Luthuli, a former Zulu chief and leader of the African National Congress, who received the 1960 prize for his peaceful efforts to end apartheid in South Africa. The struggle to end apartheid was still going on in 1964, and King acknowledged Luthuli in his acceptance speech on December 11. Recognizing also that for the 22 million blacks in the United States, the American civil rights movement was "beleaguered and committed to unrelenting struggle," King said: "I conclude that this award which I received on behalf of that movement is profound recognition that nonviolence is the answer to the crucial political and moral question of our time—the need for man to overcome oppression and violence without resorting to violence and oppression. . . . I accept this prize on behalf of all men who love peace and brotherhood."[10]

In 1965, a major dispute over voting rights broke out in Selma, Alabama. King went to Selma in January to help organize protests. He was joined by many blacks and whites from throughout the country. The demonstrators protested against the efforts of white officials there to deny most black citizens the chance to register and vote. Over the next two months, at least three people were killed and hundreds were beaten and jailed as opposition to King's campaign increased. But authorities continued to deny blacks their voting rights. King himself spent five days in jail in February and later noted, "There were many more Negroes in jail in Selma than there were Negroes registered to vote."[11] On March 7, while King was back in Atlanta conducting the Sunday worship service at his church, several hundred protesters attempted to march from Selma to Montgomery, the state capital, but police officers in Selma used tear gas and clubs to break up the group. The bloody attack, broadcast nationwide on television news shows, shocked the public. King immediately announced that another attempt would be made to march from Selma to Montgomery. On March 15, President Johnson went before the U.S. Congress to request a bill that would eliminate all barriers to Southern blacks' right to vote. On March 21, King led about 30,000 people, guarded by federal troops, on a march from Selma to Montgomery. Upon their arrival at the capital on March 25, he demanded that blacks be given the right to vote without unjust restrictions.

Largely as a result of the activities in Selma, Congress a few months later passed the Voting Rights Act of 1965. President Johnson signed it on August 6. The act outlawed the use of a poll tax or a literacy test as a requirement to vote and prohibited major changes in Southern voting laws without approval from the Department of Justice. It also provided for federal officials to supervise voter registration wherever the right to vote had been unjustly denied. The act gave the vote to thousands of Southern blacks who had never voted and eventually led to a huge increase in the number of black elected officials.

After the Voting Rights Act became law, King turned some of his attention toward other areas of concern. He was particularly troubled about the direction the United States was heading in the ongoing Vietnam War (1957–1975). When Johnson became president, U.S. forces in Vietnam consisted of about 16,300 military advisers. On Aug. 7, 1964, in response to an alleged North Vietnamese torpedo boat attack on U.S. destroyers in the Gulf of Tonkin, the U.S. Congress passed the Tonkin Gulf Resolution, which gave the president power to take "all necessary measures" and "to prevent further aggression." On March 6, 1965, President Johnson sent U.S. Marines to South Vietnam to protect U.S. bases there and to stop the North Vietnamese Communists from overrunning the country. The Marines were the first U.S. ground troops to enter the war. Johnson also ordered U.S. planes to step up bombing attacks against North Vietnam. By mid-1965, U.S. forces had reached about 60,000.

In June 1965, King received a letter from Thich Nhat Hanh, a South Vietnamese Buddhist monk, urging him to publicly oppose the war. Buddhists, who formed a majority of South Vietnam's population, had been protesting against their government since 1963 for restricting their religious practices. This appeal on religious grounds only added to King's concern. On Aug. 12, 1965, King publicly called for the United States to stop the bombing and to clearly express a willingness to negotiate a settlement of the conflict. President Johnson took umbrage at what he perceived to be King's attempt to involve himself in foreign affairs. NAACP executive secretary Roy Wilkins, fearing that an angered Johnson could turn against black leaders working for civil rights, urged King to refrain from further comments about the war. Other black leaders, white politicians, and even the press criticized King for speaking out against the war. Stung by these rebukes, King withdrew from further public comments on it.

In the meantime, a more pressing matter drew King away from the Vietnam issue. From August 11 to 15, riots raged throughout the poverty-stricken black Watts district of Los Angeles, about 10 miles

(16 kilometers) south of the city's downtown. Rioters looted and burned buildings in an outburst of racial violence that left 34 people dead and nearly 900 injured. At the invitation of local groups, King arrived on August 17 and toured the charred remains of the Watts business district, as groups of National Guardsmen posted at street corners maintained order. King saw the riots as a consequence of poverty resulting from a substandard quality of education and continued discrimination against urban blacks in jobs, housing, and law enforcement. He remarked:

> In the South there is something of shared poverty, Negro and white. In the North, white existence, only steps away, glitters with conspicuous consumption. Even television becomes incendiary when it beams pictures of affluent homes and multitudinous consumer products to an aching poor, living in wretched hovels.
>
> In these terms Los Angeles could have expected riots because it is the luminous symbol of luxurious living for whites. Watts is closer to it, and yet farther from it, than any other Negro community in the country. The looting in Watts was a form of social protest very common through the ages as a dramatic and destructive gesture of the poor toward symbols of their needs.[12]

However, understanding the cause of the violence did not mean King condoned it. On the contrary, he considered the Watts upheaval an indicator of "a crisis for the nonviolent movement."[13] King appealed to President Johnson to help Los Angeles implement programs that would raise employment and reduce poverty in the city.

In 1965, President Johnson declared that it was not enough simply to eliminate *de jure* segregation—that is, separation of the races by law. It was also necessary to end *de facto* segregation—that is, racial separation in fact and based largely on custom. The president called for programs of "affirmative action" that would offer blacks equal opportunity with whites in areas where discrimination had a long history and still existed, such as employment and education. Many businesses and schools then began to implement affirmative action programs. These programs, some of which were mandated by the federal government, gave hundreds of thousands of blacks new economic and educational opportunities.

# Chapter 4: Later Civil Rights Activities

## CHICAGO CAMPAIGN

Although the Civil Rights Act of 1964 and the Voting Rights Act of 1965 were major accomplishments of the civil rights campaign, Martin Luther King, Jr., believed that the race riots that occurred in urban areas of the North during 1964 and 1965 were an indicator that civil rights leaders should pay more attention to the economic problems of blacks. In 1966, King helped begin a nonviolent civil rights campaign in Chicago, his first major effort outside the South. King felt that to truly understand the problems of slum dwellers, one should live among them so, in January, he moved his family into a third-floor apartment at 1550 South Hamlin Avenue, in the run-down black neighborhood of North Lawndale on the West Side of Chicago. He observed firsthand the way in which many of the neighborhood's residents were trapped in a vicious circle of poverty: "You could not get a job because you were poorly educated, and you had to depend on welfare to feed your children; but if you received public aid in Chicago, you could not own property, not even an automobile, so you were condemned to the jobs and shops closest to your home. Once confined to this isolated community, one no longer participated in a free economy, but was subject to price fixing and wholesale robbery by many of the merchants of the area."[1] He noticed, for example, that the rent for his shabby, four-room apartment was $94 per month, while in some white neighborhoods, the rent was only $78 per month for a clean, newer five-bedroom apartment.

King and his SCLC associates worked with the Coordinating Council of Community Organizations (CCCO), a coalition of local civil rights groups, in the Chicago campaign. Leaders of the campaign tried to organize black inner-city residents who suffered from unemployment, rat-infested housing, poor schools, and crime-ridden streets. The leaders also protested against real estate practices that prevented blacks from living in many neighborhoods and suburbs. King believed such practices played a major role in trapping poor blacks in urban ghettos. However, Richard J. Daley, the powerful white mayor of Chicago, issued reports claiming great progress by his administration in the areas of housing and education. He actively courted the black vote, promising that federal assistance through President Johnson's Great Society programs—laws designed to help the poor and to add to the economic security of other Americans—would soon reach Chicago blacks. He argued that the poverty among Chicago's blacks originated in the South, where most of them had come from. Although King tried to promote nonviolent protest tactics throughout the campaign, race riots erupted on Chicago's West Side on July 12. Two days later, Illinois Governor Otto Kerner, Jr., called out the National Guard to quell the violence. When the local leaders of the Chicago campaign organized peaceful marches of blacks and whites through white neighborhoods, angry residents threw bottles and rocks at the demonstrators. On August 26, King met with Daley and other Chicago civic leaders, who promised to encourage fair housing practices in the city if King would stop the protests. King accepted the offer, and the Chicago campaign ended.

Some observers believed that King's Chicago campaign accomplished little. Perhaps the most successful part of it was the SCLC's establishment of a program called Operation Breadbasket. The purpose of the program was to persuade white-owned companies to hire black workers and to sell products made by black firms. Jesse L. Jackson, a local civil rights activist, became director of Operation Breadbasket in 1966. By 1967, Operation Breadbasket had branched out to 11 other cities, and the Chicago operation had successfully completed negotiations with chain grocery stores and the milk and soft drink industries.

## SHIFTS IN THE CIVIL RIGHTS MOVEMENT

By the mid-1960's, some blacks began to contend that it was nearly impossible to change white racial attitudes. They saw the civil rights movement as meaningless and urged blacks to live apart from whites and, in some cases, to use violence to preserve their rights. Two groups promoting these ideas emerged in 1966: the Black Panther Party and the Black Power Movement.

The Black Panther Party, a radical political organization, was established in Oakland, California, in 1966. Its two main founders, Huey P. Newton and Bobby Seale, had been inspired by Malcolm X, an eloquent spokesman for the Black Muslims during the 1950's and 1960's who was assassinated on Feb. 21, 1965. Another prominent leader of the Black Panthers was Eldridge Cleaver, who became a dynamic spokesman for the group. The Black Panthers promoted violent revolution as the only way to end brutal police actions and to provide economic opportunities for blacks. The Black Panthers favored the use of guns, both for self-defense and to retaliate against people believed to be oppressing the poor. Clashes between the Panthers and the police resulted in several shoot-outs.

The Black Power Movement developed after James H. Meredith, the first black student to attend the University of Mississippi, was shot during a march on June 6, 1966. As a result of this shooting and other continued racial violence in the South, SNCC chairman Stokely Carmichael, H. Rap Brown, and other members of the Student Nonviolent Coordinating Committee began to doubt the sincerity of white support for black rights. They encouraged a more aggressive response to violence against civil rights workers and called for a campaign to achieve "Black Power." They urged blacks to gain political and economic control of their own communities and to reject the values of white America and form their own standards. They emphasized the idea that "black is beautiful" and recommended that black Americans no longer refer to themselves as "colored" or "Negroes" but instead as "blacks," "African Americans," or "Afro-Americans." The Black Power Movement rejected complete nonviolence and called for blacks to respond to violence with violence. Carmichael and Charles Hamilton described the Black Power Movement in their book *Black Power,* published in 1967.

The slogan "Black Power" troubled King and many white supporters of racial equality. It seemed to many people, both black and white, that the religious, nonviolent emphasis of the civil rights movement was changing. King reiterated his commitment to nonviolence, but disputes among civil rights groups over "Black Power" suggested that King no longer spoke for the whole civil rights movement.

In 1967, King became more critical of American society than ever before. King started the year with a two-month sabbatical in Jamaica. Secluded in a cliffside villa overlooking the Caribbean Sea, he used this time to finish writing his book *Where Do We Go from Here: Chaos or Community?* In it, he reflected on the progress made in the civil rights movement since his first campaign in Montgomery back in 1955, he addressed his concerns with the approach of the Black Power Movement regarding civil rights goals yet to be achieved, and he laid out his predictions and proposals for the future of the civil rights movement.

The culmination of a decade of progress with the Voting Rights Act of 1965 marked the end of "one phase of development in the civil rights revolution," King wrote, "a struggle to treat the Negro with a degree of decency, not of equality." The subsequent second phase, implementation of programs that would bring about "the realization of equality," would be much more difficult to achieve, he added, noting that "the absence of brutality and unregenerate evil is not the presence of justice."[2] White resistance to this second phase would be harder to overcome, he contended, in part because it would require much greater monetary support: "The discount education given Negroes will in the future have to be purchased at full price if quality education is to be realized. Jobs are harder and costlier to create than voting rolls. The eradication of slums housing millions is complex far beyond integrating buses and lunch counters."[3] As a result, he lamented, progress toward true equality was moving at a much slower pace than the more basic accomplishments of the first phase.

It was no wonder blacks were getting frustrated, King acknowledged: "Cries of Black Power and riots are not the causes of white resistance, they are consequences of it."[4]

*King was arrested and jailed several times while protesting against injustice and discrimination. From a Birmingham jail in 1963, he wrote: "Injustice anywhere is a threat to justice everywhere."*

However, he asserted that blacks' loss of confidence in the white power structure to effect change was in essence "a loss of confidence in themselves" because they failed "to appreciate two important facts": (1) that "the line of progress is never straight," and (2) that "a final victory is an accumulation of many short-term encounters."[5]

Although King agreed in principle with the Black Power Movement's ideas about blacks developing pride in themselves as blacks and about increasing their political and economic control of their communities, he disagreed that real progress could be made without cooperation from whites, difficult though it might be to gain. "Like life, racial understanding is not something that we find but something that we must create,"[6] he contended. King suggested that a slogan such as "black consciousness" or "black equality" would sound less threatening to whites than "Black Power"—"and would more accurately describe what we are about."[7] He steadfastly refused to consider any course of civil rights action that allowed violence, even in self-defense, claiming that "it is dangerous to organize a movement around self-defense. The line of demarcation between defensive violence and aggressive violence is very thin."[8] But that was not his only reason. "Beyond the pragmatic invalidity of violence is its inability to appeal to conscience," King argued in his book. "Some Black Power advocates consider an appeal to conscience irrelevant. . . . But power and morality must go together, implementing, fulfilling and ennobling each other. . . . Nonviolence is power, but it is the right and good use of power."[9] Thus, he wrote, "in spite of the positive aspects of Black Power, which are compatible with what we have sought to do in the civil rights movement all along without the slogan, its negative values, I believe, prevent it from having the substance and program to become the basic strategy for the civil rights movement in the days ahead."[10]

Looking toward the future, King asserted that while it would be important for blacks to continue to increase their economic and political power, the most pressing issue to be addressed in the American civil rights movement was that of poverty, which he believed underlay many of the nation's other problems. However, King's concern about poverty extended beyond the U.S. borders.

"The time has come for an all-out world war against poverty," he declared. "The rich nations must use their vast resources of wealth to develop the underdeveloped, school the unschooled, and feed the unfed."[11] King presciently wrote in his book:

> The first step in the world-wide war against poverty is passionate commitment. All the wealthy nations—America, Britain, Russia, Canada, Australia, and those of western Europe—must see it as a moral obligation to provide capital and technical assistance to the underdeveloped areas. These rich nations have only scratched the surface in their commitment. There is need now for a general strategy of support. Sketchy aid here and there will not suffice, nor will it sustain economic growth. There must be a sustained effort extending through many years. . . . If they would allocate just 2 percent of their gross national product annually for a period of 10 or 20 years for the development of the underdeveloped nations, mankind would go a long way toward conquering the ancient enemy, poverty.[12]

King also identified two other major problems to be confronted on a global level. The first was racism. "The classic example of organized and institutionalized racism is the Union of South Africa. Its national policy and practice are the incarnation of the doctrine of white supremacy in the midst of a population which is overwhelmingly black," King wrote. As he continued in his book, he again seemed ahead of his time: "But the tragedy of South Africa is not simply in its own policy; it is the fact that the racist government of South Africa is virtually made possible by the economic policies of the United States and Great Britain, two countries which profess to be the moral bastions of our Western world."[13] The second major problem King identified was war. "A final problem that mankind must solve in order to survive in the world house that we have inherited is finding an alternative to war and human destruction,"[14] King stated. He argued, "One day we must come to see that peace is not merely a distant goal that we seek but a means by which we arrive at that goal. . . . Therefore I suggest that the philosophy and strategy of nonviolence become immediately a subject for study and for serious experimentation in every field of human conflict, by no means excluding the relationship between nations."[15] He concluded,

"We still have a choice today: nonviolent coexistence or violent coannihilation. This may well be mankind's last chance to choose between chaos and community."[16]

*Where Do We Go from Here* laid out the direction the remainder of King's own life would take. He wrapped up the book manuscript to meet his publisher's deadline of Feb. 15, 1967, and soon afterward returned to his work in the United States.

King began once again to speak out against continued U.S. involvement in the Vietnam War. This time he would not be persuaded to hold back. He addressed listeners at the Nation Institute in Los Angeles on February 25 and at the Chicago Coliseum on March 25. King was the main speaker at an antiwar program held at Riverside Church in New York City on April 4, an event attended by about 3,000 people. He followed that speech with an appearance at a huge antiwar rally at the United Nations building in New York City on April 15 that drew a crowd of more than 100,000. On May 29, he appeared in a U.S. televised interview on *Face the Nation* in which he again urged an end to U.S. bombing in South Vietnam. Many supporters of the war denounced King's criticisms, but the growing antiwar movement welcomed his comments. King's book *Where Do We Go from Here: Chaos or Community?* was published in June, and he spent most of that month on tour promoting it.

The summer of 1967 brought some good news for the civil rights movement. About the time King's book came out, Thurgood Marshall became the first black justice on the U.S. Supreme Court. An NAACP lawyer early in his career, Marshall was the primary strategist of the series of cases that ended with the Supreme Court's *Brown* school desegregation decision in 1954. President Kennedy appointed Marshall to the U.S. Court of Appeals in New York in 1961, and President Johnson named him solicitor general of the United States in 1965 before appointing him to the Supreme Court in 1967. Another encouraging piece of news came on July 6, 1967, when the U.S. Department of Justice reported that more than half of all eligible black voters were registered in Alabama, Georgia, Louisiana, Mississippi, and South Carolina.

But for the fourth year in a row, race riots flared in the heat of the summer. They raged in Newark, New Jersey, in mid-July and in Detroit, later in the month. Altogether, more than 60 people died and nearly 1,000 were injured. On June 26, King joined other black leaders in appealing for an end to the riots. President Johnson established a commission headed by Illinois Governor Kerner to study the causes of the outbreaks.

Later in the year, King prepared to act upon his conviction that poverty was as great an evil as racism. Believing that true social justice would require a redistribution of wealth from the rich to the poor, King began to plan a Poor People's Campaign led by the SCLC that would unite poor people of all races in a struggle for economic opportunity. The campaign would demand a federal guaranteed annual income for poor people and other major antipoverty laws. King envisioned this campaign as more aggressive but still nonviolent, a "mass civil disobedience"[17] that would involve sit-ins at government buildings and disruption of the traffic flow so that people would be forced to pay attention to it. The Poor People's Campaign was officially launched on December 4 during a press conference at Ebenezer Baptist Church in Atlanta.

## ASSASSINATION AND LEGACY

As 1968 began, Martin Luther King, Jr., was busy organizing the Poor People's Campaign. He planned that in late April, he would lead several thousand poor people in a march on Washington, D.C., that would culminate in a huge rally at the Lincoln Memorial with a crowd of hundreds of thousands. A second phase of the campaign would involve nonviolent sit-ins and demonstrations in the capital. Some of King's SCLC associates thought these plans were too ambitious and doubted they would succeed, but King would not be dissuaded. Meanwhile, the Vietnam War raged on. These developments contributed to King's becoming increasingly depressed and introspective as the weeks passed. In March, the Kerner Commission issued its report on the causes of the race riots of recent years. The commission placed much of the blame on racial prejudice of whites. The report stated that the average black American was still poorly housed, clothed, paid, and educated and still often suffered from segregation, police abuse, and other kinds of discrimination. The Kerner Commission recommended numerous programs to improve ghetto conditions, and it called for greater changes in the racial attitudes of white Americans. The report reinforced key points that King had made the year before in his book *Where Do We Go from Here: Chaos or Community?* But President Johnson said he thought the recommended programs would be too expensive to implement.

King went to Memphis, to support a strike of black garbage workers in mid-March. The black community's apparent willingness to engage in nonviolent demonstrations and the people's warm reception to a speech he gave helped lift some of King's depression. He decided to come back and lead a peaceful protest march in Memphis later that month. When he returned, King checked into the Lorraine Motel, a motor lodge near the waterfront, where he usually stayed while visiting Memphis. Desegregation laws notwithstanding, it was one of the few motels in town that accepted black guests. King and Ralph Abernathy, his SCLC colleague and closest friend, led off the march in downtown Memphis on March 28. But suddenly, some teen-agers at the back of the line began to smash store windows and loot the stores. What King had not known earlier was that Memphis had a gang of Black Power youths called the Invaders who were determined to sabotage the nonviolent protest. King immediately called off the rest of the march and was hustled away in a car with Abernathy, but the atmosphere descended into chaos, as police confronted the rioting youths and fired tear gas into the confused, panicked crowd. They then opened fire with guns, killing a 16-year-old black boy and injuring many others. King was heartsick when he saw the devastation on the television news and blamed himself for allowing it to happen by failing to do the proper intelligence work beforehand. He went home to Atlanta but vowed to return to Memphis, better prepared, to make another attempt at leading a nonviolent march there, later scheduled for April 8.

On March 31, President Johnson shocked the nation by announcing that he would not run for reelection. He also announced a reduction in the bombing of North Vietnam. King was buoyed by both of these announcements. He hoped that someone more responsive to the civil rights movement could be elected in the fall.

On April 3, King and Abernathy set off for Memphis again. Their flight's departure was delayed by a bomb threat, but the plane arrived in Memphis without incident. At the Memphis airport, King refused a security detail of Memphis police detectives. King and Abernathy checked in at the Lorraine Motel and took their bags up to room 306, which overlooked a courtyard with a parking lot. But Memphis detectives, FBI agents, and U.S. Army intelligence officers kept watch on King from a fire station across the street. That night, a weary King went out into a thunderstorm to address a crowd of about 2,000 supporters at the Mason Temple, the headquarters of the Church of God in Christ in Memphis. In his speech, King offered encouragement to the striking garbage workers and their families, and he urged the city's black citizens to exert economic pressure on businesses that had been unfair in their hiring policies. But toward the end of the speech, he engaged in a lengthy personal reflection on the path his life had taken, including his brush with death in the stabbing incident. He acknowledged the bomb scare and other threats that surrounded his visit to Memphis and then concluded:

> Well, I don't know what will happen now. We've got some difficult days ahead. But it doesn't matter with me now. Because I've been to the mountaintop.
>
> . . . And I've seen the promised land. I may not get there with you. But I want you to know tonight, that we, as a people will get to the promised land. And I'm happy, tonight. I'm not worried about anything. I'm not fearing any man. Mine eyes have seen the glory of the coming of the Lord.[18]

The next morning, April 4, King met with the SCLC executive staff in the Lorraine Motel conference room. King and Abernathy later ate catfish and salad for lunch at the motel. In the afternoon, King went downstairs to the room where his brother, A. D. King, was staying, and they had a pleasant visit together. Abernathy later joined them, and the three men made plans to have dinner that evening at the home of Samuel Kyles, a local black minister. About

5:00 p.m., M. L. King and Abernathy went back up to room 306 to shave and dress for dinner. Kyles arrived at the room about 5:30 to escort them. Several other SCLC members—including key aides Andrew Young, Bernard Lee, and James Bevel—milled around in the courtyard below with King's limousine driver. At about 6:00, King, Abernathy, and Kyles were ready to go. As Kyles headed downstairs to the parking lot, Abernathy decided to duck back into the room for a final splash of aftershave. King paused at the iron railing of the balcony outside room 306 to wait for his friend.

Suddenly, a loud noise crackled through the air. King was thrown backward as a bullet fired from a high-powered rifle tore into the right side of his face. It shattered his right cheek and jaw, passed through his neck, and severed his spinal cord. King grabbed his throat as he fell to the balcony floor, blood gushing from the wound. An undercover Memphis police officer reached King first and tried to stanch the flow of blood with a towel. At the sound of the gunshot, Abernathy ran from room 306 onto the balcony and bent down to cradle his fallen friend, stroking King's left cheek and telling him not to be afraid. Kyles came back up the stairs, found a blanket to cover King, and screamed into the room phone for the switchboard operator to put through a call. Others from downstairs, who had taken cover when the shot was fired, scrambled to help. Within minutes, police cars and an ambulance arrived on the scene. Abernathy rode with King in the ambulance to St. Joseph's Hospital in Memphis and stayed with him in the operating room, as a team of doctors worked desperately to save his fading life. In addition to the loss of blood, the doctors discovered that King had suffered permanent brain damage from lack of oxygen and would remain paralyzed from the neck down as a result of the spinal cord injury.

This time he would not survive. King was pronounced dead at 7:05 p.m. He was 39 years old. Coretta Scott King, home in Atlanta, had heard about the shooting and was en route to the Atlanta airport on her way to join her husband when he died.

King's assassin had fired the murder weapon across the motel parking lot from a bathroom window in a run-down boardinghouse about a block away. The rifle was found there, but the shooter had escaped. A massive federal manhunt snared the suspected sniper, a white drifter and escaped convict named James Earl Ray, a few days later.

King's assassination produced immediate shock, grief, and anger. Blacks rioted in more than 100 American cities. President Johnson declared April 7 a national day of mourning. People throughout the world mourned King's death. On April 8, the peaceful protest march that King had planned took place in Memphis, led by Abernathy, Coretta Scott King, and the three oldest King children. Between 20,000 to 40,000 people participated in the march, and there was no violence. The garbage workers' strike it supported was settled eight days later.

King's funeral was held on April 9 at Ebenezer Baptist Church in Atlanta. Nearly 800 mourners packed the church, and over 60,000 surrounded the church outdoors, listening to the service over loud-speakers. King was buried in South View Cemetery in Atlanta. His body was later moved near Ebenezer Baptist Church. King's tomb-stone bears the words: "Free at last, free at last, thank God Almighty, I'm free at last."

## AFTERMATH

King's assassination helped President Johnson persuade the U.S. Congress to approve the Civil Rights Act of 1968. The act, also known in part as the Fair Housing Act of 1968, pro-hibited racial discrimination in the sale and rental of most of the housing in the United States. In June 1968, the U.S. Supreme Court went beyond the 1968 act and ruled that a federal law passed in 1866 prohibits discrimination in the sale and rental of all property.

Ralph Abernathy succeeded King as president of the Southern Christian Leadership Conference. In May 1968, he led the "Poor People's March" on Washington, D.C., which dramatized problems faced by poor people. However, the Poor People's Campaign did not achieve the impact King had hoped for.

Coretta Scott King continued to work for civil rights. Later in 1968, she founded the King Center, an "official, living memorial" in

*Coretta Scott King, center, dressed in black, leads the "March on Memphis" on April 8, 1968, four days after the assassination of her husband. Her oldest children Yolanda, Martin III, and Dexter, walk on her right. King's SCLC successor, Ralph Abernathy walks on her left, along with Andrew Young, later U.S. President Jimmy Carter's ambassador to the United Nations and mayor of Atlanta.*

Atlanta that includes exhibits, archives, and a library. The book *The Trumpet of Conscience,* a collection of radio addresses by Martin Luther King, Jr., was published posthumously in 1968, with an introduction written by Coretta. She also wrote her own book, *My Life with Martin Luther King, Jr.,* published in 1969.

In March 1969, James Earl Ray pleaded guilty to King's murder. He was convicted of the crime and sentenced to 99 years in prison. Ray later tried to withdraw his plea, but his conviction was upheld. At the time of King's death and for years afterward, some people suspected that Ray had not acted alone in plotting King's assassination. In 1978, a special committee of the United States House of Representatives reported the "likelihood" that Ray was aided by others. Ray died in 1998. In 2000, the U.S. Justice Department announced that an 18-month investigation of King's death had turned up no evidence of a conspiracy.

In 1974, King's mother was shot and killed in Atlanta while playing the organ at Ebenezer Baptist Church. The gunman, Marcus

Wayne Chenault, was a member of a small religious cult that opposed black Christian ministers. Chenault received the death penalty, but in 1995, he was resentenced to life in prison without parole. King's father died of a heart attack in 1984.

In 1977, King was posthumously awarded the Presidential Medal of Freedom. The Martin Luther King, Jr., National Historic Site was established in 1980. It includes more than 20 buildings in Atlanta's Sweet Auburn neighborhood. King's birthplace, church, and burial place are all part of the historic site. In 1991, the National Civil Rights Museum opened in Memphis at the site of King's assassination.

In 1983, the U.S. Congress established a legal federal holiday honoring King's birthday. Martin Luther King, Jr., Day was first celebrated on Jan. 20, 1986, and is observed each year on the third Monday in January. Today, the holiday is also observed as a state holiday by all 50 states. Most government offices, banks, and schools are closed on Martin Luther King, Jr., Day. After George Washington, the nation's first president, King became only the second American whose birthday is observed as a national holiday.

King's writings continue to be published. A single volume titled *A Testament of Hope: The Essential Writings of Martin Luther King, Jr.,* was published in 1986. A more extensive collection, *The Papers of Martin Luther King, Jr.,* began publication in 1992 with the first of 14 planned volumes. Subsequent volumes were released in 1994, 1997, 2000, and 2005.

On May 2, 1994, Coretta Scott King had the pleasure of hearing her late husband's famous words "Free at last! Free at last!" echoed by the newly elected black president of South Africa, Nelson Mandela, as she stood nearby on the podium at his victory celebration.

Coretta Scott King tirelessly continued her husband's work until a heart attack and stroke in 2005 left her partially paralyzed and unable to speak. She made her last public appearance on Jan. 14, 2006, at a Salute to Greatness dinner as part of Martin Luther King, Jr., Day celebrations in Atlanta. Coretta Scott King died on Jan. 30, 2006, at age 78. ■

# Nelson Mandela (1918– )

Nelson Mandela *(man DEHL uh)* became an international symbol of the struggle for racial justice. Born into the black majority population of South Africa at a time when the country was ruled by a white minority, Mandela spent most of his life fighting for a democratic society in which people of all races would have equal rights and opportunities. Like such civil rights leaders as Mohandas K. Gandhi of India and Martin Luther King, Jr., of the United States, Mandela was arrested and jailed as a result of his protest activities. Mandela was imprisoned for 27 years. After his release, he led negotiations with white leaders that eventually brought an end to the South African white-minority government's policy of rigid racial separation. He went on to win the Nobel Peace Prize and become the first black president of South Africa.

## EARLY LIFE

Nelson Mandela was born on July 18, 1918, in the tiny riverside village of Mvezo near Umtata in the Transkei territory (now the South African province of Eastern Cape). At that time, the territory was part of the Union of South Africa, a self-governing country within the British Empire. His name at birth was Rolihlahla Mandela. In his autobiography, Mandela recalled that *Rolihlahla* in his native Xhosa language literally means "pulling the branch of a tree," adding that a looser but more accurate translation would be "troublemaker."

Mandela's father, Gadla Henry Mphakanyiswa, was a chief of the Xhosa-speaking Tembu ethnic group. His mother, Nosekeni Fanny, was third of his father's four wives. (Many peoples in Africa practice *polygamy,* a system in which a man is married to more than one woman at the same time.) Each wife had her own *kraal,* a social unit within the village characterized by a homestead consisting of several round thatched huts, a fenced-in enclosure for animals, and fields for growing crops. Young Rolihlahla had three sisters, Baliwe, Notancu, and Makhutswana; six half sisters; and three half brothers.

In 1919, a white local magistrate summoned Mandela's father to settle a dispute about an ox that had strayed from its owner. The chief, a proud, stubborn man, believed that the magistrate had no legitimate authority in tribal matters and refused to come. But the constitution of the Union of South Africa gave whites almost complete power. The offended magistrate promptly charged the chief with insubordination and deposed him. Deprived of most of his land and cattle and the income they generated, Gadla moved his family to the nearby village of Qunu, where Nosekeni had friends and relatives. The Xhosas of Qunu continued to regard Mandela's father as royalty and treated the family with great respect.

Mandela spent much of his early childhood herding cattle and farming. The family ate mostly corn, sorghum, beans, and pumpkins grown on the farm and drank milk from their cows. Rolihlahla sometimes caught fish from the cool streams nearby or knocked birds from the sky with a slingshot. He spent his free time playing in the grassy open spaces and foothills with the other boys of the village, and he became skilled at stick-fighting. As his mother prepared supper in a three-legged iron pot over an open fire at the kraal, she enraptured the children with Xhosa legends and fables that had been passed down for many generations. After befriending a pair of African Christians in Qunu, Mandela's mother became a Methodist and had her son baptized.

At the age of 7, Mandela became the first member of his family to attend school, proudly wearing a pair of his father's cut-off trousers in place of the traditional Xhosa boy's clothing of a blanket wrapped around one shoulder and pinned at the waist. The British-trained African teacher at the one-room, Western-style schoolhouse gave each pupil an English name. As Mandela recalled in his autobiography, "Africans of my generation—and even today—generally have both an English and an African name. Whites were either unable or unwilling to pronounce an African name, and considered it uncivilized to have one. That day, Miss Mdingane told me that my new name was Nelson."[1]

In 1927, when Mandela was 9 years old, his father died of lung disease. Mandela's mother then took him on a long journey by foot to Mqhekezweni, the Tembuland capital in the Transkei. They went to the Great Place of Chief Jongintaba Dalindyebo, the acting *regent* (ruler) of the Tembu people, who had offered to become the boy's guardian and raise him as a son. Mandela continued his studies in a one-room schoolhouse next door to the palace, where his courses included geography, history, English, and Xhosa. Mandela was a diligent student. Outside of school, he rode horses and worked as a plowboy, a wagon guide, or a shepherd. He also enjoyed boxing and long-distance running. Mandela attended Methodist church services every Sunday with Dalindyebo's family.

Young Mandela was a keen observer of the regent's court. Meetings were called as needed to discuss particular matters, and all Tembus were free to attend. Anyone who wished to speak was allowed to do so without interruption. The regent, who sat quietly through all the speeches, even permitted the speakers to criticize him. A large banquet was served during the day. Then the meeting continued until a *consensus* (agreement in opinion) was reached. "Unanimity, however, might be an agreement to disagree, to wait for a more propitious time to propose a solution," Mandela recalled. "Democracy meant all men were to be heard, and a decision was taken together as a people. Majority rule was a foreign notion. A minority was not to be crushed by a majority."[2] Finally, at the end of the day, the regent spoke. He attempted to sum up what had been said throughout the day and form a consensus among the various opinions expressed. If no agreement could be reached, another meeting would be held. The gathering ended with lively entertainment by a poet or singer. These meetings had a profound impact on Mandela. They fueled his desire to claim his right to his father's chieftaincy and its accompanying power. They also contributed greatly to the development of his general philosophy of leadership.

## MANHOOD AND COLLEGE

As Mandela reached his teens, he grew tall, like his father. When he was 16 years old, Mandela and his brother participated along with 24 other boys in the traditional Xhosa circumcision ritual that represented their entry into manhood. As part of the ritual, he was given the additional *circumcision name* of Dalibunga, meaning "founder of the Bungha." The Bungha was the ruling council of the Transkei. At a subsequent ceremony to officially welcome the 26 new men into society, Mandela received two heifers and four sheep—the first property he ever owned. But then the regent's son Chief Meligqili, the keynote speaker, shocked the audience by asserting that the Xhosa and all black South Africans were slaves in their own country. Meligqili's words rang in Mandela's ears: "The abilities, the intelligence, the promise of these young men will be squandered in their attempt to eke out a living doing the simplest, most mindless chores for the white man. These gifts today are naught, for we cannot give them the greatest gift of all, which is freedom and independence." Mandela thought Meligqili was "an ignorant man" and considered him "enormously ungrateful"[3] for the education and other benefits the white colonizers had brought to South Africa. It was not until much later that Mandela appreciated what a visionary Meligqili had been.

Soon after the manhood ceremony, Mandela's guardian enrolled him at the Methodist Clarkebury Boarding Institute in Engcobo to be educated in preparation for becoming counselor to the king. There he met students from other parts of the Transkei and from Johannesburg. Several years later, in 1937, he entered Healdtown, the Methodist college in Fort Beaufort. Both of these schools were patterned after British boarding schools. Although Mandela absorbed a great deal about British culture, he retained a strong sense of personal identity as "a Xhosa first and an African second."[4] He graduated from Healdtown in 1938.

In 1939, Mandela entered South African Native College (now the University College of Fort Hare), the only black university in South Africa at that time. His courses included anthropology, English, politics, and law. He competed in soccer and cross-country running, joined the drama society, and learned ballroom dancing. As a member of the Students Christian Association, he taught Sunday school classes in nearby villages. Through soccer and the Christian group, he became acquainted with a fellow student, Oliver Tambo, whom he would later get to know better. Mandela followed with interest the developments of World War II (1939–1945), which South Africa had entered on Sept. 6, 1939, on the side of the British against Nazi Germany.

Mandela's second year of college at Fort Hare started off well. He was nominated as a candidate for the Student Representative Council (SRC). At a meeting of the entire student body, however, the students voted to boycott the upcoming SRC election unless the administration agreed to improve the school's food service and increase the SRC's power. The administration refused the students' demands, and nearly all of them boycotted the election. Mandela supported the boycott. After he was elected by the few who did vote, he resigned. For thus acting "irresponsibly,"[5] Mandela was expelled in 1940. He returned to Mqhekezweni, where an unpleasant surprise awaited him. The regent had decided it was time for Mandela to marry, had chosen him a bride, and made all the arrangements. The woman was dignified but fat and Mandela was not attracted to her. Considering the idea of this marriage unfair, Mandela ran away to Johannesburg, leaving behind his dream of succeeding his father as a Xhosa chief.

## LAW CAREER AND FIRST MARRIAGE

Johannesburg was a city of more than a million people, and its population surged in the early 1940's as black laborers streamed in from the countryside to fill jobs vacated by white workers, who were fighting overseas in the war. Well-educated, ambitious black young people also migrated from rural areas to Johannesburg to take advantage of opportunities provided by the booming wartime economy. This influx of black Africans alarmed the city's white *Afrikaners*—that is, descendants of Dutch farmers (originally known as *Boers*) who began settling in the area in the mid-1600's. Afrikaner nationalism had been on the rise throughout the 1920's and 1930's. In 1931, South Africa gained full independence as a member of the Commonwealth of Nations, an association of the

United Kingdom and some of its former colonies. Afrikaners gained control of the government and passed restrictive laws that made life more difficult for the country's black Africans, Indians, and other nonwhite groups. Although the South African government needed the support of the nation's nonwhite majority during the war, the increase in nonwhite workers also increased Afrikaner nationalists' fear of the "black peril" and would soon lead them to call for more extreme separation of the country's racial groups.

Upon arrival in Johannesburg in 1941, Mandela got a job as a policeman at Crown Mines. But his career at the mines was cut short when the regent discovered his whereabouts and ordered that he be sent home. Mandela fled to Alexandra, a black township north of Johannesburg, where he met Walter Sisulu, a businessman and community leader from the Transkei. Sisulu helped Mandela get a job as a clerk for a white lawyer, Lazar Sidelsky, a partner in one of Alexandra's largest law firms. Mandela studied law by correspondence course and went on to work for three other white law firms before becoming a lawyer himself. In 1952, Mandela opened South Africa's first black law partnership with his old college classmate Oliver Tambo.

In 1944, Mandela married Sisulu's cousin Evelyn Ntoko Mase, a nurse, in a simple civil ceremony. Their first son, Madiba Thembekile, known by the nickname Thembi, was born in 1945. A daughter, Makaziwe Phumla, was born in 1947 but died after nine months. A second son, Makgatho Lewanika, was born in 1950. A second daughter, born in 1953, was named Makaziwe in the cultural tradition of honoring a deceased child's memory.

## AFRICAN NATIONAL CONGRESS (ANC) ACTIVITY

Under the "wise tutelage" of Walter Sisulu, Mandela slowly gravitated toward political activism. As Mandela reflected in his autobiography,

*I cannot pinpoint a moment when I became politicized, when I knew that I would spend my life in the liberation struggle. To be an African in South Africa means that one is politicized from the moment of one's birth, whether one acknowledges it or not. . . .*

*[An African's] life is circumscribed by racist laws and regulations that cripple his growth, dim his potential, and stunt his life.*

*I had no epiphany, no singular revelation, no moment of truth, but a steady accumulation of a thousand slights, a thousand indignities, a thousand unremembered moments, produced in me an anger, a rebelliousness, a desire to fight the system that imprisoned my people. There was no particular day on which I said, From henceforth I will devote myself to the liberation of my people; instead, I simply found myself doing so, and could not do otherwise.*[6]

Sisulu introduced Mandela to the African National Congress (ANC), an organization founded in 1912 to work for black African rights. In August 1943, Mandela participated along with thousands of others in a boycott of public bus service in Alexandra to protest a fare increase. The strike was organized by the Zulu activist Anton Lembede, who sought to bring a more populist appeal to the traditionally middle-class, conservative ANC. After the buses ran empty for nine days, the previous fare was restored. Mandela joined the ANC in early 1944. In April of that year, Mandela, Sisulu, Tambo, and others helped form the ANC's Youth League, with Lembede as its president.

After World War II (1939–1945), South Africa became a founding member of the United Nations (UN). But within South Africa, there was no peace. In 1946, about 70,000 black African miners went on a nonviolent strike for higher pay and better working conditions. After about a week, however, the mine owners, supported by government police, brutally forced the workers back into the mines and prosecuted the leaders of the miners' union. Also in 1946, the South African government passed the Asiatic Land Tenure Act, which severely restricted the rights of Indians to buy property and limited where they could live and trade. In response to this act, which the Indians called the Ghetto Act, the Indian community launched a two-year campaign of passive resistance modeled after the earlier campaigns of the great Indian leader Mohandas K. Gandhi. Mandela was impressed by the Indians' willingness to suffer, sacrifice, and even go to jail for their beliefs. India's independence from the United Kingdom on Aug. 15, 1947, showed Africans how a ruling power could be defeated by an organized, unified mass movement.

In 1948, the Afrikaner-led National Party came to power. It instituted a policy called *apartheid (ah PAHRT hayt),* under which racial groups were legally segregated and given different rights and privileges. The word *apartheid* means *separateness* in the Afrikaner language of Afrikaans. Apartheid classified each South African by race into one of four categories: (1) black; (2) white; (3) *Coloured*—that is, mixed race; or (4) Asian, which included Indians. The policy required segregation in housing, education, employment, transportation, and public accommodations. Apartheid limited the rights of nonwhites to own or occupy land or to enter white neighborhoods. The South African government tried to justify apartheid by claiming that people of different races could peacefully coexist only if the races were separated from one another. However, white South Africans used apartheid mainly to control the nation's huge nonwhite majority.

After the South African government established apartheid, Mandela and others in the Youth League believed the time had come for the ANC to instigate mass action similar to the nonviolent protests used successfully in India by Gandhi, whose assassination in 1948 had shocked Mandela. In 1949, the Youth League drafted a Program of Action calling for boycotts, strikes, "stay-at-homes," noncooperation, protest demonstrations, and other forms of *civil disobedience*—that is, the deliberate and public refusal to obey a law. The ANC adopted this program of nonviolent tactics, calling for equality for all races and leading open resistance to the government. On June 26, 1950, the ANC joined with Indian and Communist groups to stage a political strike called the National Day of Protest. In the cities, most workers stayed home, and black businesses were closed for the day.

Early in 1952, Mandela and several other black and Indian leaders began to organize a widespread campaign of civil disobedience called Defiance Against Unjust Laws to protest six specific apartheid laws. The organizers decided to model the campaign after Gandhi's *Satyagraha* campaigns of nonviolent resistance. A practical strategist, Mandela recalled his view at the time: "I saw nonviolence in the Gandhian model not as an inviolable principle but as a tactic to be used as the situation demanded. . . . I called for non-violent protest for as long as it was effective."[7] The Defiance campaign began on June 26, 1952. Over the next six months, more than 8,000 black, Coloured, and Indian volunteers peacefully broke the law by committing such acts as entering white neighborhoods, walking into whites-only railroad compartments, or staying out after curfew. Mandela and about 50 volunteers spent two days in jail at a police station for being out after curfew the first night of the campaign. It was Mandela's first "concentrated experience"[8] of imprisonment, and he was appalled at how callously the white guards treated the prisoners. Mandela himself received a kick in the shin for complaining about it. Later that year, Mandela was sentenced to a nine-month suspended jail sentence and a six-month ban on attending any meetings of any kind or even talking to more than one person at a time. He was not allowed to leave Johannesburg without permission. The Defiance campaign overall yielded mixed results. It attracted a great deal of popular support and boosted membership in the ANC. However, none of the six targeted laws was repealed, and the government passed further legislation to stiffen the penalties for deliberate lawbreaking to include *flogging* (beating as punishment) and longer jail sentences. The struggle was far from over.

As soon as the six-month ban expired, Mandela went back to the weekly ANC meetings. Soon he was slapped with another ban, this time for two years, and forced to resign from the ANC. But he secretly continued to work for the ANC. In 1955, he helped draft the Freedom Charter, a manifesto calling for equal rights for all of South Africa's people. On Dec. 5, 1956, the government charged Mandela and 155 other antiapartheid leaders of all races with treason. They were detained in the Johannesburg Prison for two weeks before being released on bail. The trial dragged on for several years. Mandela provided his own defense. On March 29, 1961, all 156 of the accused antiapartheid leaders were found not guilty.

Even before Mandela's arrest for treason, his political activism was beginning to take its toll on his marriage. He usually left for work at his law office early in the morning and attended ANC meetings in the evening, returning home late at night. Evelyn became involved with the Jehovah's Witnesses (a Christian religious group that believes in one God, called Jehovah), and soon her devotion to religion matched Nelson's to politics. But neither spouse was fully supportive of the other's dedication. Their relationship cooled, and after several separations, they divorced in 1957. That year, Nelson met a young social worker named Winifred Nomzamo Madikizela, known as Winnie, and quickly fell in love with her. They were married on June 14, 1958. The couple would have two daughters: Zenani (called Zeni), born Feb. 4, 1959; and Zindziswa (called Zindzi), born Dec. 23, 1960. Winnie enthusiastically supported Nelson's political activity and later became an activist in her own right.

In 1959, some black Africans who opposed the ANC's alliances with white groups left the ANC and formed the Pan-Africanist Congress (PAC), which favored the establishment of an all-black government. PAC organized a peaceful protest against the apartheid laws that required black Africans to carry *passes* (identity papers). On March 21, 1960, protesters throughout the country gathered at police stations without their passes, thus inviting arrest. In most places, the police dispersed the crowd without incident. But at Sharpeville (now part of Vereeniging), near Johannesburg, police opened fire on the protesters and killed 67 black Africans. The Sharpeville massacre set off rioting and demonstrations throughout South Africa and prompted a wave of international protest against the South African government. The government outlawed both the PAC and the ANC, but Mandela renewed the protests and went into hiding to avoid arrest.

In the wake of the Sharpeville massacre, Mandela became convinced that nonviolent resistance was no longer an effective strategy for dealing with a government that did not hesitate to respond with violence. With ANC approval, Mandela in 1961 founded a separate guerrilla organization called *Umkhonto we Sizwe* (Spear of the Nation), which became known by the abbreviation MK. He spent months researching South Africa's past, learning about armed struggles in other parts of Africa, and studying the tactics of such non-African revolutionaries as Fidel Castro and Che Guevara in Cuba, Mao Zedong in China, and Menachem Begin in Israel.

From a farmhouse in Rivonia, near Johannesburg, where he lived under an assumed name, Mandela on June 26 sent a letter to South African newspapers that concluded, "Only through hardship, sacrifice, and militant action can freedom be won. The struggle is my life. I will continue fighting for freedom until the end of my days."[9] On December 16—a day Afrikaners celebrated for a bloody battle in 1838 in which the Boers triumphed over the Zulus—MK exploded homemade bombs at government offices and electrical power stations in Johannesburg, Durban, and Port Elizabeth. Suddenly whites and blacks alike understood that black resistance had reached a new level. MK set off another round of explosions on New Year's Eve and continued its campaign of sabotage against government buildings throughout 1962. Altogether, Umkhonto we Sizwe claimed responsibility for more than 70 acts of sabotage. Mandela sneaked out of the country a number of times to meet with foreign political leaders in other parts of Africa and in England and to arrange for arms shipments to MK. But on Aug. 5, 1962, the police finally caught up with Mandela in Durban and arrested him.

*Mandela is shown in 1961 at age 42.*

## IMPRISONMENT

Mandela was charged with incitement to strike and with leaving the country without a passport. He was held in prison until his trial began on Oct. 22, 1962, in Pretoria. That day he wore a Xhosa leopard-skin garment as a representation of the history, culture, and heritage of his people. Mandela conducted his own defense throughout the trial and concluded with an eloquent speech in which he reiterated his determination to continue the fight for a democratic society in South Africa. On November 7, he was convicted on both charges and sentenced to five years in prison.

In July 1963, while Mandela was in prison serving his five-year sentence, police raided the farmhouse in Rivonia, capturing Sisulu and collecting hundreds of incriminating documents about MK operations, some of them in Mandela's own handwriting. With this new evidence against him, Mandela was brought to trial on a new charge of sabotage. This time he was defended by his own specially chosen team of lawyers. Mandela's testimony included a four-hour speech explaining the development of his political ideas and his choice to resort to sabotage after nonviolent forms of protest had failed to effect social change. He concluded:

> During my lifetime I have dedicated myself to this struggle of the African people. I have fought against white domination, and I have fought against black domination. I have cherished the ideal of a democratic and free society in which all persons live together in harmony and with equal opportunities. It is an ideal which I hope to live for and achieve. But if needs be, it is an ideal for which I am prepared to die.[10]

On June 11, 1964, Mandela and seven other antiapartheid leaders were convicted of sabotage. The next day, they were sentenced to life in prison. One of the men, a white Communist named Dennis Goldberg, was taken to a white jail in Pretoria. Mandela and the others—Sisulu, Govan Mbeki, Raymond Mhlaba, Andrew Mlangeni, and Elias Motsoaledi, who were all black Africans, and Ahmed Kathrada, an Indian—were shipped to the Robben Island prison fortress off the coast of Cape Town.

At Robben Island, Mandela and his fellow prisoners were kept isolated from the outside world. They were denied access to newspapers or radio and at first could only write and receive one letter every six months. The prisoners were given only cold water for bathing, and their diet consisted mainly of a "pap" (porridge) made from corn. They slept on thin straw mats on the stone floor. Mandela's cell measured about 8 feet (2.4 meters) by 7 feet (2.1 meters) and had a small window with iron bars and a view overlooking the courtyard. Mandela was housed with a group of about 30 political prisoners, including ANC and PAC members who had been convicted in other trials, in a cell block away from the general prison population out of concern that the political prisoners might stir up trouble among the others. However, this arrangement helped Mandela maintain contact with his ANC friends and buoyed his spirit.

Mandela spent many years at hard labor in the prison's limestone quarry, but he was invigorated by the 20-minute walk and preferred hauling rocks outdoors to being cooped up in the prison courtyard. Mandela resisted bullying by the white warders and insisted on being treated with dignity. Sometimes he was punished with a few days of solitary confinement for standing up to the guards. Eventually the prisoners were allowed to have books for academic study and, on rare occasions, visitors. Winnie Mandela visited her husband whenever she could. At home, she endured almost constant police harassment as she became a leading spokesperson for her husband's cause. As news from the outside world filtered in, Nelson Mandela followed the struggle of black Americans against racism, discrimination, and economic inequality in addition to the struggles of his own people, which included violent clashes in the summer of 1976 following an incident in Soweto when police opened fire on children in a protest march. Two collections of Mandela's speeches and writings were published while he was at Robben Island: *No Easy Walk to Freedom* (1965) and *The Struggle Is My Life* (1978, rev. ed. 1986, 1990).

In 1982, to weaken the ANC power base, Mandela was transferred to the maximum-security Pollsmoor Prison outside Cape Town and kept mostly in isolation for six years. It was the same prison where Gandhi had first been placed in solitary confinement, and Mandela expressed "a bond between us." At Pollsmoor, Mandela had a real bed, better food, a rooftop garden to work in, and weekly letters and half-hour visits from Winnie. But he was still a prisoner.

While imprisoned, Mandela became a symbol of the struggle for racial justice. In the mid-1980's, black protesters staged numerous labor strikes, demonstrations, and riots. At the same time, military branches of the ANC and PAC carried out guerrilla attacks on government targets. On Jan. 31, 1985, South African president P. W. Botha publicly offered to release Mandela if he "unconditionally rejected violence as a political instrument." As he had done earlier with several privately issued conditional offers, Mandela refused. His daughter Zindzi read his public response on February 10 in which he challenged Botha to "renounce violence," "dismantle apartheid," and lift the ban on the ANC, and he assured the people, "Your freedom and mine cannot be separated."[11] On June 12, 1986, the South African government declared a national state of emergency under which it could arrest and hold people without charging them. But the violence continued. Later that year, the European Community, the Commonwealth of Nations, and the United States enacted *sanctions* (bans) on certain kinds of trade with South Africa. Botha had realized since the 1970's that apartheid was causing South Africa's economy to suffer, and the sanctions made the situation even worse. The South African government repealed the pass laws and the laws prohibiting interracial marriage, but black Africans were still excluded from participation in government.

By 1986, Mandela had decided it was time to try requesting private talks with the South African minister of justice, Kobie Coetsee, about ways to secure the unconditional release of political prisoners and to devise some sort of compromise between the government and the ANC, neither of which was willing to engage in direct negotiation with the other while the ANC was banned. In 1987, Coetsee and Mandela had the first of about a dozen meetings over the span of three years. In July 1988, over the objections of the South African government, a rock concert in London celebrating the imprisoned Mandela's 70th birthday was broadcast to 200 million television viewers in 60 countries, increasing his international fame. The worldwide mood of celebration turned to concern the following month when Mandela was diagnosed with tuberculosis. The disease was successfully treated, and about four months later Mandela returned from Tygerberg Hospital and Constantiaberge Clinic to his imprisonment. This time he was placed in a whitewashed, one-story house with a swimming pool and shade trees in the yard—surrounded by a concrete wall topped with razor wire, with guards posted at the front door—on the grounds of Victor Verster prison in Paarl, near Cape Town.

In 1989, after Botha suffered a stroke, F. W. de Klerk became president of South Africa. De Klerk realized that white minority rule could not continue without great risk of civil war. That October, he unconditionally released Sisulu and six other political prisoners from Robben Island. In December, he sent for Mandela, and the two men had a cordial discussion. Mandela urged de Klerk to lift the ban on the ANC and all other political organizations, end the state of emergency, release political prisoners, and allow exiles to return. In early February 1990, de Klerk ended the state of emergency and lifted the bans on political organizations, including the ANC and PAC.

Finally, on the afternoon of Feb. 11, 1990, Nelson Mandela walked through the front gates of Victor Verster, a free man after 27 years in prison. Hand-in-hand with Winnie, Mandela raised his clenched right fist in the ANC salute to the waiting crowd. Television cameras broadcast his unconditional release around the world.

*Mandela and his second wife Winnie walk in the gardens at the residence of South African civil rights leader and Anglican Archbishop Desmond Tutu in February 1990, the day after Mandela was released from prison. Married in 1958, the couple were divorced in 1996.*

## END OF APARTHEID

After leaving prison, Mandela agreed to suspend the armed struggle the ANC had been waging against the South African government. Over the objections of more radical ANC members, he urged conciliation with de Klerk and other government leaders. Mandela sought to obtain political power for the country's blacks in a peaceful way. In May 1990, the South African government held its first formal talks with the ANC. Mandela met with de Klerk several times after that to discuss political change in South Africa. In 1990 and 1991, the government repealed most of the remaining laws that had formed the legal basis of apartheid. But Mandela also negotiated an end to other forms of racial injustice, including laws that denied blacks the right to vote in national and provincial elections. In 1991, the government, the ANC, and other groups began holding talks on a new constitution. That year, Mandela was elected head of the ANC.

Mandela's reintegration into family life proved more difficult than his reentry into public life. Relationships with his wife and children lacked the kind of passion he brought to his work. Within the ANC, Winnie had become popular, especially among younger members, but also increasingly militant. In 1991, she was convicted of kidnapping in connection with a group that abducted four young men and murdered one of them. Nelson supported his wife throughout the four-month trial, but eventually he found their personal and political differences too difficult to live with. On April 13, 1992, he read a public statement announcing the couple's separation. They were divorced in March 1996.

In 1993, the South African government adopted an interim constitution that gave the nation's blacks full voting rights. Mandela and de Klerk won the 1993 Nobel Peace Prize in recognition of their work to end apartheid and to enable the country's nonwhites to fully participate in the South African government. On April 27, 1994, South Africa held its first truly open national elections in which all races could vote. The ANC won nearly two-thirds of the National Assembly seats, and the Assembly elected Mandela president. At a victory celebration on May 2, Coretta Scott King, the widow of the slain American civil rights leader Martin Luther King, Jr., appeared on the podium with Mandela as he echoed the words of her late husband's most famous speech in proudly acknowledging "the joy that we can loudly proclaim from the rooftops—Free at last! Free at last!"[12]

## PRESIDENT OF SOUTH AFRICA

On May 10, 1994, Nelson Mandela was sworn in for a five-year term as president of South Africa. He was the nation's first black president. Mandela's two *deputy presidents* (vice presidents) were the former president de Klerk and Thabo Mbeki, an ANC member and ally of Mandela's former law partner, Oliver

Tambo. Acting on his belief that "the liberation struggle was not a battle against any one group or color, but a fight against a system of repression," Mandela reached out to Afrikaners in a spirit of reconciliation. In June 1995, his popularity increased among white sports fans—whose teams had been kept from international competitions by antiapartheid boycotts—when he personally presented the World Cup rugby trophy to the victorious South African team at the end of its thrilling championship match on a field in Johannesburg. The team's members were all Afrikaners except for one Coloured. Mandela also attempted to build consensus with Indians and other minority groups. He described his efforts in his autobiography *Long Walk to Freedom,* published in 1994 after he became president. "At every opportunity," he recalled, "I said all South Africans must now unite and join hands and say we are one country, one nation, one people, marching together into the future."[13]

As president, Mandela launched the Reconstruction and Development Programme to improve living conditions throughout the country. He also worked to reestablish diplomatic and economic ties with nations that had broken off relations with South Africa

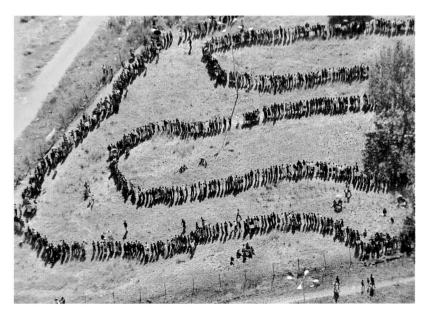

*Mandela negotiated an end to many forms of racial injustice, including laws that denied blacks the right to vote in national and provincial elections. The first truly open national elections in which all races could vote were held in April 1994 and drew long lines of voters to the polls. The ANC won a majority of the seats in the country's National Assembly, and Mandela became president.*

*Mandela and President F. W. de Klerk of South Africa shared the 1993 Nobel Peace Prize. They were honored for their work to end apartheid and to enable the country's nonwhites to fully participate in the South African government.*

because of apartheid. On June 23, 1994, South Africa was readmitted to the United Nations after 20 years of exclusion.

In 1995, Mandela's government appointed a panel called the Truth and Reconciliation Commission to gather information about human rights abuses during the apartheid years. Desmond Tutu, a black African retired Anglican archbishop and winner of the 1984 Nobel Peace Prize, headed the commission. It issued a report in 1998 in which it found that the apartheid-era government had committed "gross violations of human rights," including kidnapping and murders. But the report also criticized the ANC and other opposition groups, holding them responsible for some killings and torture.

South Africa adopted a new Constitution in 1996. It provides for a strong presidency and includes a wide-ranging bill of rights for all citizens.

Mandela resigned as head of the ANC in 1997. Mbeki was elected to succeed him. On July 18, 1998—his 80th birthday—Mandela married Graca Machel, the widow of President Somora Machel of Mozambique.

Mandela retired as president of South Africa shortly before the elections in June 1999. The ANC won a majority in the National Assembly, and the Assembly elected Mbeki president.

## LATER YEARS

Although he was no longer an elected official, Mandela remained active in world affairs. In July 1999, he served as a mediator in peace talks between the Hutu and Tutsi ethnic groups in Burundi. In 2000, he facilitated negotiations between Libya and Western powers regarding the 1988 explosion of an American airliner over Lockerbie, Scotland, as a result of bombs planted on the plane by Libyan terrorists. In 2002, Mandela criticized the attitude of the United States toward Iraq and called the U.S. attitude a threat to world peace. A U.S.-led coalition of forces, including British troops, invaded Iraq in March 2003. In a speech to the South African Parliament on May 10, 2004, Mandela condemned the United States and the United Kingdom for their role in the Iraq War.

In July 2003, Mandela launched a major effort to fight the AIDS epidemic in South Africa, where more than 10 percent of the population is infected with HIV, the virus that causes the disease. Mandela's son Makgatho died of AIDS on Jan. 6, 2005. Later that year, Mandela hosted a series of rock concerts in South Africa and other countries to raise money for helping South African women with HIV. Mandela also made appeals to leaders of the Group of Eight (G8)—an informal organization of eight major industrialized nations, including the United States and the United Kingdom—to support a plan to reduce poverty in Africa. In July 2005, the G8 announced it would increase economic aid to Africa and cancel debt obligations of some poorer African nations. ■

*Mandela speaks at the launch of the first public-private partnership HIV/AIDS treatment facility in Cape Town, South Africa, in December 2003. Ten percent of the population of South Africa is infected with HIV, the virus that causes AIDS.*

# Notes

## MOHANDAS K. GANDHI

1. Mohandas K. Gandhi, *An Autobiography; or, The Story of My Experiments with Truth*, Transl. by Mahadev Desai, 2nd ed. (1940; Boston: Beacon Press, 1993) 25.
2. Gandhi, *Autobiography* 28.
3. Gandhi, *Autobiography* 112.
4. Gandhi, *Autobiography* 172.
5. Gandhi, *Autobiography* 189.
6. Gandhi, *Autobiography* 299.
7. Gandhi, *Autobiography* 301.
8. Yogesh Chadha, *Gandhi: A Life* (New York: Wiley, 1997) 125–126.
9. Gandhi, *Non-Violent Resistance (Satyagraha)* (1951; Mineola, NY: Dover Publications, 2001) 1.

## MARTIN LUTHER KING, JR.

Introduction

1. Mahatma Gandhi, *The Essential Gandhi: An Anthology of His Writings on His Life, Work, and Ideas*, ed. Louis Fischer (1962; New York: Vintage Spiritual Classics, 2002) 280.

Chapter 1

1. Martin Luther King, Jr., *The Autobiography of Martin Luther King, Jr.*, ed. Clayborne Carson (New York: Warner Books, 1998) 6. Copyright © 1998 by The Heirs to the Estate of Martin Luther King, Jr. Reprinted by arrangement with the Estate of Martin Luther King, Jr., c/o Writers House as agent for the proprietor New York, NY.
2. King, *Autobiography* 8.
3. King, *Autobiography* 7.
4. King, *Autobiography* 7.
5. Stephen B. Oates, *Let the Trumpet Sound: A Life of Martin Luther King, Jr.* (New York: HarperPerennial, 1994) 16.
6. King, *Autobiography* 9–10.
7. King, *Autobiography* 10.
8. King, *Autobiography* 11.
9. King, *Autobiography* 11–12.
10. King, *Autobiography* 14.
11. King, *Autobiography* 14.
12. Martin Luther King, Jr., "Kick Up Dust," letter to the editor, *Atlanta Constitution*, 6 Aug. 1946. Qtd. in King, *Autobiography* 15.
13. King, *Autobiography* 15.
14. King, *Autobiography* 16.
15. King, *Autobiography* 17.
16. King, *Autobiography* 18.
17. King, *Autobiography* 18.
18. King, *Autobiography* 20.
19. King, *Autobiography* 23.
20. King, *Autobiography* 24.
21. King, *Autobiography* 26.
22. King, *Autobiography* 26.
23. King, *Autobiography* 32.
24. King, *Autobiography* 34.
25. King, *Autobiography* 35.
26. Qtd. in Taylor Branch, *Parting the Waters: America in the King Years, 1954-63* (New York: Simon & Schuster, 1988) 95–96.
27. King, *Autobiography* 35.
28. King, *Autobiography* 44–45.

Chapter 2

1. King, *Autobiography* 52.
2. King, *Autobiography* 55.
3. Branch 135.
4. King, *Autobiography* 55.
5. Qtd. in David J. Garrow, *Bearing the Cross: Martin Luther King, Jr., and the Southern Christian Leadership Conference* (New York: Morrow, 1986) 321.
6. Martin Luther King, Jr., "Meaning of the Boycott," *New York Times*, 24 Feb. 1956. Qtd. in King, *Autobiography* 81.
7. "The South: Attack on the Conscience," *Time*, 18 Feb. 1957: 17.
8. King, *A Testament of Hope: The Essential Writings of Martin Luther King, Jr.*, ed. James M. Washington (San Francisco: Harper & Row, 1986) 197–198.
9. Oates 136.
10. Carson 118.
11. King, *Autobiography* 134.
12. King, *Autobiography* 141.

Chapter 3

1. King, *Autobiography* 173.
2. King, *Autobiography* 181.
3. King, *Testament of Hope* 290.
4. King, *Testament of Hope* 298.
5. King, *Testament of Hope* 302.
6. Excerpted from "I Have a Dream" by Martin Luther King, Jr. Copyright © 1963 by Martin Luther King, Jr.; copyright renewed 1991 by Coretta Scott King. Reprinted by arrangement with the Estate of Martin Luther King, Jr., c/o Writers House as agent for the proprietor, New York, NY.
7. King, *Autobiography* 231–232.
8. Oates 275.
9. Oates 306.
10. King, *Testament of Hope* 224, 226.
11. King, *Autobiography* 276.
12. King, *Testament of Hope* 192.
13. King, *Autobiography* 296.

Chapter 4

1. King, *Autobiography* 301.
2. King, *Testament of Hope* 557.
3. King, *Testament of Hope* 558.
4. King, *Testament of Hope* 562.
5. King, *Testament of Hope* 562–563.
6. King, *Testament of Hope* 572.
7. King, *Testament of Hope* 574.
8. King, *Testament of Hope* 590.

9. King, *Testament of Hope* 592.

10. King, *Testament of Hope* 582.

11. King, *Testament of Hope* 624.

12. King, *Testament of Hope* 624.

13. King, *Testament of Hope* 621.

14. King, *Testament of Hope* 626.

15. King, *Testament of Hope* 627–628.

16. King, *Testament of Hope* 633.

17. Michael E. Dyson, *I May Not Get There with You: The True Martin Luther King, Jr.* (New York: Free Pr., 2000) 86.

18. King, *Testament of Hope* 286.

### NELSON MANDELA

1. Nelson Mandela, *Long Walk to Freedom: The Autobiography of Nelson Mandela* (Boston: Little, Brown, 1994) 12.

2. Mandela, *Long Walk* 19.

3. Mandela, *Long Walk* 26.

4. Mandela, *Long Walk* 37.

5. Mandela, *Long Walk* 45.

6. Mandela, *Long Walk* 83.

7. Mandela, *Long Walk* 111.

8. Mandela, *Long Walk* 115.

9. Mandela, *Long Walk* 236.

10. Mandela, *The Struggle Is My Life* (New York: Pathfinder, 1986) 181.

11. Mandela, *Long Walk* 454–455.

12. Mandela, *Long Walk* 540

13. Mandela, *Long Walk* 540.

# Recommended Reading

## BOOKS

Branch, Taylor. *Parting the Waters: America in the King Years, 1954–63.* New York: Simon & Schuster, 1988.

Branch, Taylor. *Pillar of Fire: America in the King Years, 1963-65.* New York: Simon & Schuster, 1998.

Burns, Stewart. *To the Mountaintop: Martin Luther King Jr.'s Sacred Mission to Save America, 1955-1968.* San Francisco: HarperSanFrancisco, 2004.

Carson, Clayborne, et al., eds. *The Papers of Martin Luther King, Jr.* 5 vols. to date. Berkeley: Univ. of Calif. Pr., 1992.

Chadha, Yogesh. *Gandhi: A Life.* New York: Wiley, 1997.

Dyson, Michael E. *I May Not Get There with You: The True Martin Luther King, Jr.* New York: Free Pr., 2000.

Fairclough, Adam. *To Redeem the Soul of America: The Southern Christian Leadership Conference and Martin Luther King, Jr.* 1987. Athens: Univ. of Ga. Pr., 2001.

Fischer, Louis. *The Life of Mahatma Gandhi.* New York: Harper, 1950.

Gandhi, Mohandas K. *An Autobiography; or, The Story of My Experiments with Truth,* Transl. by Mahadev Desai, 2nd ed. 1940. Boston: Beacon Press, 1993.

—. *Non-Violent Resistance (Satyagraha).* 1951. Mineola, NY: Dover Publications, 2001.

Garrow, David J. *Bearing the Cross: Martin Luther King, Jr., and the Southern Christian Leadership Conference.* New York: Morrow, 1986.

Hansen, Drew D. *The Dream: Martin Luther King, Jr., and the Speech That Inspired a Nation.* Ecco-Pr., 2003.

Hardiman, David. *Gandhi in His Time and Ours: The Global Legacy of His Ideas.* New York: Columbia Univ. Pr., 2003.

Johnson, Charles R., and Adelman, Bob. *King: The Photobiography of Martin Luther King, Jr.* New York: Viking Studio, 2000.

King, Martin Luther, Jr., *The Autobiography of Martin Luther King, Jr.,* ed. Clayborne Carson. New York: Warner Books, 1998.

Mandela, Nelson. *Long Walk to Freedom: The Autobiography of Nelson Mandela.* Boston: Little, Brown, 1994.

—. *The Struggle Is My Life.* New York: Pathfinder, 1986.

Meredith, Martin. *Nelson Mandela: A Biography.* New York: St. Martin's, 1997.

Oates, Stephen B. *Let the Trumpet Sound: The Life of Martin Luther King, Jr.* 1982. New York: HarperPerennial, 1994.

Sampson, Anthony. *Mandela: The Authorized Biography.* New York: Knopf, 1999.

Siebold, Thomas, ed. *Martin Luther King, Jr.* San Diego: Greenhaven, 2000.

## WEB SITES

*The King Center.* <http://www.thekingcenter.org/tkc/index.asp>

"The Official Mahatma Gandhi eArchive & Reference Library." Mahatma Gandhi Foundation-India, <http://web.mahatma.org.in/index.jsp>

"The Nobel Peace Prize - Laureates." Official Web site of the Nobel Foundation, <http://nobelprize.org/peace/laureates/#top> Includes biographies of King and Mandela.

"Martin Luther King, Jr., National Historic Site." National Park Service, U.S. Dept. of the Interior. <http://www.nps.gov/malu/>

"The *Time* 100: The Most Important People of the Century." <http://www.time.com/time/time100/> Includes profiles of Gandhi, King, and Mandela.

# Glossary

**affirmative action** any plan or program that promotes the employment of women and of members of minority groups.

**Afrikaner** *(AF ruh KAH nuhr)* a white person born in South Africa of European, especially Dutch or Huguenot, ancestry; Boer.

**ahimsa** *(uh HIHM sah)* the doctrine of nonviolence.

**apartheid** *(ah PAHRT hayt or ah PAHRT hyt or ah PAHRT hyd)* racial segregation, especially as formerly practiced in the Republic of South Africa.

**ashram** *(AH shruhm)* a small rural retreat for meditation.

**Bhagavad-Gita** *(BUHG uh vuhd GEE tah)* a Sanskrit philosophical dialogue of about A.D. 1 in which Krishna (Bhagavat) is identified with the Supreme Being, and expounds the duties and customs that are basic to Hinduism.

**boycott** to refuse to buy or use a product or service.

**Brahman** *(BRAH muhn)* a member of the priestly caste, the highest caste in India.

**caste** *(kast or kahst)* one of the social classes into which Hindus are divided. By tradition, a Hindu is born into the caste of his father and cannot rise above it.

**civil disobedience** refusal because of one's principles to obey the laws of the country or state, especially by not paying taxes or by refusing to serve in the armed forces.

**civil rights** the rights of a citizen, especially those guaranteed to all citizens of the United States, regardless of race, color, or sex, by the Bill of Rights, the 13th, 14th, 15th, 19th, 24th, and 26th amendments to the United States Constitution, and certain acts of Congress.

**desegregation** *(dee SEHG ruh GAY shuhn)* the doing away with the practice of providing separate schools and other public facilities for racial groups, especially blacks and whites.

**integration** *(IHN tuh GRAY shuhn)* the inclusion of people of all races on an equal basis in neighborhoods, schools, parks, or other facilities.

**Jim Crow law** a law that discriminates against black people, especially in traditional institutions or by legal sanction.

**Kshatriya** *(KSHAT ree yuh)* a member of the military caste, the second of the four great castes or classes among the Hindus.

**mahatma** *(muh HAHT muh or muh HAT muh)* a wise and holy person who has extraordinary powers.

**pacifism** *(PAS uh fihz uhm)* the principle or policy of universal peace; settlement of all differences between nations by peaceful means; opposition to war.

**Satyagraha** *(SUHT yuh GRUH huh)* a policy of passive resistance and withdrawal of cooperation with the state, begun by Mohandas K. Gandhi and his followers in India 1919 as a protest against certain abuses.

**segregation** *(SEHG ruh GAY shuhn)* the separation of one racial group from another or from the rest of society, especially in schools, theaters, restaurants, and other public places and private places of meeting.

**sit-in** a form of protest in which a group of people enter a public place and remain seated for a long period of time. Sit-ins are organized to protest racial discrimination, government policies, etc.

**Sudra** *(SOO druh)* a member of the lowest of the four major Hindu castes. Sudras include artisans, laborers, and servants.

**untouchable** a Hindu belonging to the lowest caste in India, whose touch supposedly defiled members of higher castes.

**Vaisya** *(VYS yuh)* a member of the mercantile and agricultural caste among the Hindus.

**varna** *(VAHR nuh)* any one of the four main castes or classes of Hindu society: the *Brahmans* (priests and scholars), the *Kshatriyas* (rulers and warriors), the *Vaisyas* (merchants and professionals), and the *Sudras* (artisans, laborers, and servants).

# Index

Page numbers in *italic* type refer to pictures.